RUNE CASTING

OBSERVATIONS FROM A MODERN LENS

THEMES OF ANIMISM, SOUND, & MANIFESTATION

KARIN DAHLSTROM
AKA RUNE GUIDANCE OF THE NORSE

TLS

ISBN13: 978-1-959350-60-6

Set in: Georgia 11pt, Bodoni 72 Smallcaps 15/18pt, Great Scholar 15pt, Magical Font 24pt

©The Three Little Sisters
USA/CANADA

CONTENTS

DEDICATION AND ACKNOWLEDGMENTS

Dedication:

I dedicate this book to my students, without whom I would not be here today. You mean the world to me, and I thank you for allowing me to be your student.

To my family, living and dead. You are my very heartbeat. I love you all more than words will ever convey.

To my faithful clients. Your confidence in me has many times given me strength.

Lastly to Melina, for always believing in me our entire lives, no matter what I did.

Acknowledgements:

To the scholars who unbeknownst to them have been a positive influence in my life, I am eternally grateful for your inspiration:

Maria Kvilhaug, Professor Henrik Williams, Rune Rasmussen and Mathias Nordvig.

And to my mentors in Sweden and Norway. Tusen tack. Thank you for all your priceless lessons:

Bobby, Patrik, Max, Peter, Lennart and Johannes
Tack så mycket

PREFACE

Upon being invited to compose this work, while excited, I had some internal reservations. Traditionally, the arcane knowledge of runes has been cloaked in secrecy, a reverence echoed in the Old Norse term for the word rune itself: "secret" or "mystery." Odin's injunction in the Hávamál to maintain silence on matters of rune lore (stanza 80), underscores this guarded tradition. Similarly, in Scandinavian folk magic traditions, of which I am a practitioner, there is an emphasis on silence when cultivating and executing one's magical prowess. Staying quiet, "tyst" is essential for one's implementations to thrive.

A second Internal conflict stemmed from the inherently subjective nature of rune magic, casting and interpretation. While the Elder Futhark provides a foundational framework, its twenty-four symbols remain veiled in ambiguity. It's even possible that additional, undiscovered runes existed. The historical record offers tantalizing glimpses, but the comprehensive understanding of their application by the ancient Germanic peoples remains elusive. This text endeavors to reconcile personal experience and observations with established scholarship, presenting a nuanced perspective on rune casting and the Elder Futhark runic system. There are several reasons why my focus will be on this runic script. First, it is our oldest known rune script. Second, since there are 24 characters in it, it is easier to interpret rune castings due to having more character options to illuminate while divining. Lastly, it is the runic script that most practitioners are familiar with.

Years ago, before I opened my spiritual practice, I traveled to Sweden often for my work as an artist and to visit friends and family. It was during these oversea adventures that I fostered a profound connection to what I respectively call Nordic "shamanism" and the rune tradition. This foundation, coupled with my experiences as a teacher of Scandinavian folk practices, animism and rune reading, informs my approach. I have come to perceive runes as more than mere glyphs; they are representatives of living entities and land connectedness, pulsating with vital energy. While runes have had very real negative associations with hate communities the past one hundred years, their existence predates such idiocy, ignorance and misplaced accolades to romanticized nationalism and deluded Viking "culture."

It Is my sincere hope that this exploration of the runes and rune casting proves a valuable companion on your own spiritual odyssey.

In addition, I hope this book will instill in readers a renewed sense of hope and positive connection to the world through the runes. By understanding them as channels to ancient wisdom and an animistic outlook, we can foster healing within ourselves, our society, and the modern world.

CHAPTER 1: RELATIONSHIPS

"And some things that should not have been forgotten were lost. History became legend. Legend became myth."
- J.R.R. Tolkien,Fellowship of the Ring, 1954

In the hushed depths of a pre-Viking Scandinavian longhouse, an old crone is hunched by a fire, her silhouette etched in the dancing firelight. On the white rabbit fur laying before her, she cast tiny, weathered objects, their edges are worn and surfaces smoothed by hands that used them for generations. The flickering flames accentuate the wrinkles on her time worn face. Long, smoke-kissed braids framed her weathered visage, a testament to countless winters endured. Crackling blaze illuminates the small pieces of wood, bone and stone, carved with familiar symbols, unfurled on the ground. Imbued with powerful energy that connects her to these objects of divination, these runes are in a relationship with her. With practiced precision, she scatters the pieces, creating a pattern only she could decipher. A silent dialogue commences, as if the objects whispered secrets to the wind, and she, a vessel, received their message. Bound by an unseen thread to the past, present, and future, she delves into the tapestry of existence, seeking answers in the heart of the fire.

Although this scenario is completely fictional, it offers a plausible glimpse into potential events. Many cultures used casting with divinatory objects as a way to connect with the divine. Just as seiðr traditions and lore have been passed down and reconstructed for new generations, so has the modern practice of rune casting. It is essential, however, to acknowledge the complex and often problematic legacy associated with runic history and it's modern divination practices. The 19th-century Romantic movement ignited a wave of nationalism, leading to a romanticized and distorted revival of 'Viking' culture across Northern Europe. This resurgence of cultural heritage took on an unsettlingly fervent and exclusive character that effected rune lore and accuracy to this day. This phenomenon has been disturbingly mirrored in the United States since the 2010s and onward.

As traditions evolve, it is imperative to critically examine their origins and to acknowledge the limitations of our understanding. The rampant misinformation surrounding runes and divination over the past century cannot be overstated. While acknowledging this historical distortion, we must also confront the contemporary reality that has emerged. Runes are indeed employed for divinatory purposes, a practice that has grown significantly despite its lack of historical foundation. It is essential to dispel the myth of an ancient, formalized system dedicated to rune divination. The esoteric use of runes was cloaked in secrecy throughout antiquity, leaving us with limited historical evidence. With this understanding, we can approach the runes with a clear perspective, recognizing their potential for contemporary application while acknowledging the absence of a concrete historical precedent. By doing so, we open ourselves to the possibility of harnessing the energies inherent in these symbols for modern-day guidance and insight.

The interpretation of runes, both individually and in combination, constitutes a longstanding ancestral practice in numerous Scandinavian households. Perhaps to my immigrant family members, runes were offering comfort amidst the challenges of a new land. Protective talismans were not uncommon in our home. They were a silent, constant presence, rather than a subject of discussion. Runes adorned inherited, ancestral hand woven tapestries, hundreds of years old, that furnished my family's abode. Everywhere I looked, protective symbols were inscribed on my environs. In my home, rune magic and religious beliefs were not contradictory to one another. One merely seemed to be an extension of the other. This melding of modern and bygone philosophies is something many of us can relate to today. Often the topic of runes divides people firmly into various camps.

The following synthesis of ideas will reconcile contemporary perspectives on runes with the constraints of historical evidence. In this book I will be focusing on the use of the Elder Futhark script as a rune casting divinatory method.

The Elder Futhark was primarily used by the early European Germanic peoples during the Migration Period, roughly from the 2nd to the 8th centuries AD or CE respectively. It consists of twenty-four symbols or letters. The name "Futhark" is derived from the first six runes: Fehu, Uruz, Thurisaz, Ansuz, Raidho, and Kenaz. While previously only thought of as a writing system to many, now it is believed that the Elder Futhark also held significant cultural and spiritual meaning for Germanic peoples. Though runes were used for the practical recording of names, dates and events, many Northern Europeans of that time also believed that runes possessed magical properties. Ritual practices, magic charms and divination often featured runes in their execution, leaving the user with a sense of power and fulfillment. Having a deeper connection to the land than many of us do today, old world Europeans depended on their relationships with nature and its symbols to work through problems such as illness, crop fertility and weather.

It's important to note that pre-Christian Scandinavians had an animistic world view. Animism can be defined as an anthropological construct, used to describe what always has existed since the beginning of our time; our relationship to the physical & non physical world. It's the concept of the immaterial soul. Although each culture has its own mythologies and rituals, animism is said to describe the most common, foundational thread of ancient and indigenous peoples' spiritual or supernatural perspectives. The animistic perspective is so widely held and inherent to most indigenous & ancient world peoples that they often didn't even have a word in their languages that corresponds to it.

In Norse culture, the natural world was revered and held a significant place in the hearts and minds of its people. Rituals and sacrifices were often performed in its honor. The Old Norse worldview was essentially a cyclical one. Creation, after the flow and balance of life, would end in destruction. Then, from the ashes of Ragnarok, a new world would arise again. This cyclical nature reflected the Norse people's deep connection to the natural world and its rhythms. One must understand this crucial concept when working with the runes and as a key component while comprehending their purpose. The Elder Futhark exemplifies these cycles of nature.

To the Old Norse speakers, everything in the natural world most likely was believed to possess a soul or spirit, and while it's not explicitly stated in the surviving texts, there are strong indications of animistic beliefs intertwined with the broader Norse religion. Norse mythology is replete with beings associated with natural elements. Animism defines the relationships with these elements. In fact, all Norse magic and divination leads back to that one word; relationships. Our relationship with our environment, our culture, our past experiences and with the runes themselves. All Nordic animism and Scandinavian folk practices have "relationship" as the foundation from which out of everything else springs.

We build relationships with the things around us, with nature, with people, with objects, with spirits and likewise, so we should build relationships with the runes before we try to yield their power or energy. We are admonished by Óđin in the Hávamál:

Do you know how to carve them?
Do you know how to read them?
Do you know how to blood them?
Do you know how to test them?
Do you know how to invoke them?
Do you know how to blót?
Do you know how to cast them?
Do you know how to sacrifice them?
-Hávamál: Stanza 144

The emphasis here, in my opinion, is on "Do you know." Knowing the runes implies having a relationship with them.

When runic divination is approached from this angle, It inserts authenticity. One's own relationships and experiences are massively important to the effectiveness of our intentional workings. Magic and interpretation become more real through this authentic acknowledgment. There is a power in this subjective truth that only the diviner can rely on, just as one would in any relationship. This is my personal philosophy regarding rune casting and rune magic.

My family held a profound reverence for ancestors, believing them to be intermediaries between the physical and spiritual realms. To honor and revere our departed family members was considered paramount to navigating earthly challenges. I was instilled with the belief that the deceased possessed the ability to intervene on our behalf, influencing benevolent spirits and deities to extend their grace, wisdom and support to the living.

For thousands of years human communities passed on wisdom, knowledge and love to the generations that came after them. This often included spiritual rituals and ancient practices that benefited each new generation. This deep, winding thread connected families through time and experience. Unfortunately, this beautiful ribbon has been severed for many. In our modern era, religious and political upsets and shifts have caused the loss of this informational exchange. Loss of relationship. As Western religion spread across the globe, many old pagan rituals and practices were lost. Pressure from political and religious authorities replaced, often forcibly, the ways we connected to this information. Many times we only see ancestral veneration and wisdom passed down and exchanged in indigenous communities globally. These indigenous communities retained what many have lost. In the western world in particular, where we have an epidemic of dysfunctional consumer culture, there has been a breach, a wound, so deep that it has severed many from their ancestral connection. A rupture has taken place that disconnects us from the land, our ancestors and from one another. Today several of us are teaching others how to connect with and honor ancestral wisdom, helping all to heal from this wound. Repairing our relationship with the Earth, with each other and with ancestral knowledge is the healing balm that all communities need to bring balance to our world.

Runes, because of their ambiguity, allow space for authentic interpretations and actually demand relationships from us by their very nature.

In the Old Norse language the word "rune" means secret or mystery. I've spent half my lifetime working with this esoteric technique, and I have come to understand some of the mysteries behind these symbols. In my opinion, the runes are energetic entities that communicate on a deep spiritual, psychological and subconscious level. Their otherworldly power is great, and being in relationship with them is a breathtaking responsibility. While some approach runic divination with skepticism, to me it is logical that we should take an atavistic approach to the runes. Given their importance, it can be deduced that they most certainly were used for divination, at least by some. In the following chapters we'll discuss further how to develop a relationship with the Elder Futhark and how it can begin to speak to you through rune casting.

Let's first take a closer look at the animistic core of Norse culture more deeply. The cornerstone of Norse belief was an intimate, interwoven relationship with the natural world. This animistic perspective, where everything possesses a spirit or soul, permeated every aspect of life. From the towering mountains to the bountiful fjords, from the icy winter winds to the flowering spring meadows, the Norse people saw not just inanimate objects, but sentient beings deserving of reverence. Their deities, often linked to natural phenomena, were seen as powerful manifestations of these spirits. Thor, the god of thunder, embodied the raw energy of storms, while Freya, associated with love and fertility, represented the life-giving power of the earth and its fruitfulness.

This animistic worldview was a reflection of the natural world's rhythms. The Norse cosmos was in constant flux, from the creation myth of the world emerging from the primordial ice to the apocalyptic vision of Ragnarok, followed by rebirth. This understanding of the cycles of life and death informed their rituals and ceremonies, their art, and their approach to life. Ancient Scandinavians didn't "believe" in magic, it just was. It simply was a fact of life and how their world worked. From the baking of bread to the plowing of a field, it all involved the supernatural. It is within this framework that the runes, as potent symbols of the cosmos, hold their significance and power.

The Elder Futhark, the ancestral rune alphabet, is more than a mere writing system. It is a microcosm of the universe, representing the fundamental forces and energies that shape reality. Each rune is a glyph imbued with the essence of specific natural elements, concepts, or deities. For instance, the rune Fehu is often associated with cattle and wealth, symbolizing the life-sustaining power of nature. The runes represent these kinds of pictorial images in the Old Norse mind.

To the Norse, working with runes was not simply a matter of interpretation but a form of communion with the natural world. By understanding the runes, one was, in essence, gaining insight into the language of the cosmos. This is why a deep connection to nature was considered essential for effective rune work. It allowed practitioners to attune themselves to the subtle energies and patterns underlying reality, enabling a more profound understanding of the runes' meanings. The same is true for us today.

Over millennia, the intricate tapestry of Norse beliefs and practices was gradually eroded with the advent of monotheistic religion. Its emphasis on a singular, omnipotent deity, challenged the polytheistic worldview. The oral traditions that preserved ancestral knowledge were disrupted, and the animistic perspective, once central to life, became marginalized, however not totally forgotten.

In recent decades, there has been a resurgence of interest in this ancestral knowledge. People are seeking reconnection with their roots, exploring ancient wisdom, and rediscovering the power of nature. This revival is not merely a nostalgic pursuit but a recognition of the enduring value of the animistic worldview. By re-establishing a relationship with the natural world, we can tap into a wellspring of wisdom and resilience. To work effectively with the runes, we must approach them with reverence and respect. This involves cultivating a deep connection to the land, spending time outdoors, observing the cycles of the seasons, and developing a sense of awe for the natural world. It is also essential to study Norse mythology and cosmology to gain a deeper understanding of the cultural context in which the runes were created.

As we explore the depths of these ancient symbols, we are also embarking on a journey of inner exploration and healing. The runes can serve as mirrors, reflecting back to us our own strengths, weaknesses, and potential. By embracing the animistic perspective and cultivating a deep connection to nature, we can unlock the full power of the runes and use them as a tool for personal growth, spiritual development and mending the ruptures in our lives. Every rune cast is like a ritual. Rituals offer a safe and sacred space to express and release suppressed emotions. This can lead to catharsis and emotional healing for communities and individuals. Ceremonies and rituals can help people find meaning and purpose in their lives especially during difficult times. Similar to meditation or prayer, rune casting is a ritualized method for tapping into a higher consciousness and is essentially a spiritual sacrament that employs symbols to access deeper insights and guidance. Ultimately, working with the runes is a journey of self-discovery, fostering a deeper understanding of one's place in the world.

CHAPTER 2: RUNES IN HISTORY:
EARLIEST ECHOES OF THE ELDER FUTHARK

The Elder Futhark, originally only accepted as a script by academics, left its mark on the annals of history in the form of enigmatic artifacts. To truly understand these symbols, we must embark on a journey back to the dawn of their existence, when the first runes began to take shape in our consciousness.

While the Elder Futhark is undeniably Germanic in character, its precise origins remain shrouded in mystery. Theories abound, with some scholars suggesting influences from Etruscan or Greek alphabets, while others propose a more organic development within Germanic cultures. Whatever the case, we can look at the tangible evidence we have found in precious artifacts. Although this book isn't a definitive historical resource on rune usage, I will provide some examples. The most obvious of these objects among the earliest evidence of the Elder Futhark are the renowned runestones. These imposing monoliths, carved with intricate runes, have provided invaluable insights into the lives, beliefs, and societies of our Northern European ancestors. While many of these stones date from later periods, some exceptional finds have pushed the boundaries of our understanding.

The Svingerud stone is currently considered the oldest known rune stone. Discovered in Norway in 2021, this sandstone slab is estimated to be between 1 and 250 AD/CE. This incredible piece pushes back the timeline of rune usage by several centuries. Something many of us believed all along. As archaeological discoveries are ongoing, it's important to note that while this is the oldest known rune stone, it's possible that even older ones await discovery. Previously, many viewed the Kylver Stone as our oldest example of use of the complete Elder Futhark. The Kylver Stone is a significant archaeological find from Sweden, dating back to around 400 AD/CE. Discovered in 1903 on the island of Gotland, it's renowned for being the oldest known example of an inscription containing the entire Elder Futhark, the earliest form of the runic alphabet. Originally used as a grave marker, the stone bears runes on its underside, reinforcing the runes' aptitude for mystery and proficiency in matters of obscurity.

Runestones are not the sole repositories of early runic inscriptions. A plethora of other artifacts have yielded crucial information. Some other incredible finds include the Vimose Comb, which also places the use of runes at a much earlier date than previously thought. Discovered in a Danish bog, this artifact dates back to the 2nd century CE. Though short and enigmatic, it represents a groundbreaking discovery. Its inscription, though challenging to decipher, offers modern rune enthusiasts tantalizing clues about the language and script of its time. Many other personal belongings such as brooches, amulets, as well as combs, have been found with runic inscriptions, providing glimpses into the lives of individuals from different social classes and strata. Incredible specimens such as swords, spears, and other weapons bearing runic inscriptions offer insights into the war culture of the time.

Bracteates, thin gold foil objects often decorated with intricate designs, have also been found with runic inscriptions, providing valuable insights into early Germanic culture, also challenging our previous timelines of runic use. The Skrydstrup bracteate is a gold artifact discovered in Skrydstrup, Denmark dating back to approximately 400-650 CE. This intricate piece of jewelry features a depiction of a god, believed to be either Odin or Tyr, accompanied by symbols such as a wolf, stag, intertwined snakes, and two birds. The bracteate offers valuable insights into the Norse mythology and artistic styles of the period.

Everyday objects like pottery and wooden utensils, when adorned with runes, reveal the extent to which this script and its possible magical intentions permeated Nordic society.

Even the most basic carvings, like a simple name, have been discovered. For example, the name 'Halfdane' was etched into the marble parapets of the Hagia Sophia in Constantinople. It's believed to have been inscribed by someone serving in the Varangian Guard during the Viking age. This generally accepted Viking graffiti shows how practical runes could be.

Often though, these inscriptions are fragmentary, weathered, or carved in cryptic styles making their study difficult and challenging. Furthermore, the limited linguistic data from this period can hamper interpretation. However as technology advances, new methods for analyzing and deciphering runes are being developed. With each new discovery and breakthrough, our knowledge of the Elder Futhark expands, moving us beyond the limited view of runes as merely a script or "alphabet." Every new find brings us increasingly closer to unraveling the mysteries of our ancestors.

Runes In Norse Sources

While the explicit mention of using runes for magical or divination purposes may not be found in all sources, several sagas, eddas, and other ancient texts reference the association between runes and magic. It should be noted that while the Norse sagas were primarily written down in the 13th century AD, the runic script referred to would likely be the Younger Futhark which was primarily used during the Viking Age, roughly 8th to 11th centuries AD. Here are some notable sources for you to expand your knowledge further:

1. The Hávamál: This poem in the Poetic Edda contains a section known as "Rúnatal," or "Lay of the Runes." In it, Odin claims to have discovered the runes after a self-sacrifice, and he describes the magical properties and uses of the runes. We will go over this section of the Hávamál more in depth in chapter 3.

2. The Saga of the Volsungs: This saga features a scene where the hero Sigurd carves runes on his sword, Gram, to invoke the magical powers of the runes and gain victory in battle.

3. The Saga of the People of Laxardal: In this saga, the character Bolli Bollason, under the guidance of a seiðkona, or seidr woman, inscribes runes on a wooden staff to help him with an upcoming conflict.

4. The Saga of the Greenlanders: This saga includes instances where runes are used in divination and prophecy. Thorbjorg, a prominent seiðkona, reads the runes to provide insights and predictions.

5. Various Skaldic Poetry: Skaldic poetry composed by medieval Norse poets often incorporates runic symbolism or emphasizes their magical qualities. Although not narrative sagas or eddas, these poems reinforce the association between runes and magic in Norse literature.

It's important to note that while these sources imply the magical significance of runes, they don't provide detailed instructions or practices for rune magic, such as rune casting. The exact methods practitioners used in ancient Norse society are not explicitly described. Modern interpretations and practices of runic magic draw from these sources, archaeological findings, and other historical research to reconstruct runic magic traditions in contemporary contexts. That being said, there is a respected tradition of rune reading and rune casting passed down in families that has been used for decades, maybe even centuries. However, it is impossible to ignore the distortions that plagued the esoteric community in the 20th century. A dangerous trend emerged as individuals sought to manipulate narratives to align with nefarious political agendas, casting a long shadow over the genuine practices of rune magic and divination. We must acknowledge such atrocities in order to free ourselves of limiting beliefs and ignorance.

RUNE SCRIPTS

While there are differences of opinion on the exact number of runic alphabets, the most commonly known Germanic rune scripts can be generalized into four basic categories:

THE ELDER FUTHARK

The oldest form of the runic alphabet. Used primarily from around the 2nd to 8th centuries AD/CE. Consisting of 24 runes.

F u T \a r k w

h n l j l p z s

t b e m l N d o

THE YOUNGER FUTHARK

A simplified version of the Elder Futhark. Used from approximately the 8th to 12th centuries AD/CE. Consisting of 16 runes. These runes were further divided into several subsets such as Danish Long-Branch Runes and the Swedish-Norwegian Short-Branch Runes. Icelandic and Saxon runes usually fall under this category as well as Staveless Runes or Hälsinge from the Hälsingland region of Sweden.

Younger Futhark	ᚠ f	ᚢ u/v/w, y, o, ø	ᚦ þ, ð	ᚬ ą, o, æ	ᚱ r	ᚴ k, g, ŋ	—	—		ᚼ/ ᚽ h	ᚾ/ ᚿ n	ᛁ i, e	ᛅ/ᛆ a, æ, e	—	—		ᛦ ʀ	ᛋ/ ᛌ s	ᛏ/ ᛐ t, d	ᛒ b, p	—	ᛘ m	ᛚ l	—	—	—

MEDIEVAL RUNES

A later form of the Younger Futhark used from the 12th to 15th centuries AD/CE. While runes were a common script in Scandinavia for centuries, their use gradually declined with the spread of Christianity and the adoption of the Latin alphabet.

abcdþðefghiklmnopqrstuvyzæø

DALECARLIAN RUNES

Many do not realize that runes were used in the countryside in Sweden even up until the early 20th century. Communities in western Sweden, such as Dalarna province, continued to use runes as recently as the early 1900s. This unique preservation of the runic script offers invaluable insights into the evolution of language and culture in the region. Known as Dalecarlian Runes, it has its own regional subset named after the isolated community of Älvdalen. Over time, the runes underwent local adaptations, leading to unique variations within different regions.

It's important to note that while they are derived from the Elder Futhark, the rune forms and their usage in Dalarna Sweden, and in Älvdalen in particular, developed unique characteristics over time, setting them apart from other runic scripts. These regionally specific runes were deeply intertwined with local folklore and beliefs, often used for divination and magical practices. Despite their isolation, the Älvdalen runes in particular, provide a fascinating glimpse into the evolution of the Germanic languages and the enduring power of tradition.

RUNE POEMS

Runic poems have also provided another crucial avenue for understanding runic scripts. These poetic compositions, scattered across Northern Europe, offer unique insights into the language, culture, and beliefs of their creators. By examining the ways in which runes are employed within these verses, scholars have been able to decipher their meanings and reconstruct the development of runic alphabets over time. Offering intriguing glimpses into the cultures that produced them, rune poems and their cryptic verses are invaluable for understanding the beliefs, values, and worldview of early Germanic peoples.

From the enigmatic inscriptions found in Scandinavia such as the Danish, Norwegian, and Swedish poems, as well as the more stylized Icelandic and Anglo-Saxon Futhorc poems, these works often incorporate the runic alphabet itself as a structural element, lending a mystical quality to their content. Used as memory aids that helped users recall the order and names of each letter in the Runic alphabet, rune poems served as a repository of significant cultural knowledge for the reader.

The Anglo-Saxon, Norwegian, Icelandic and Swedish poems have survived and date before the 20th century. Much of the knowledge and definitions attributed to the runes today come from these preserved poems. While many rune poems remain a mystery, scholars have managed to decipher some, revealing themes of heroism, fate, and the natural world. From their humble beginnings as tools for communication, runes evolved into potent symbols carrying deep cultural and spiritual connotations.

This transition from practical script to magical artifact laid the groundwork for the rich tapestry of beliefs and practices surrounding runes that would flourish in later centuries. The rune's origins are so ancient and distant that a fascinating mythology has grown around it. Shrouded in antiquity, the rune's birth has given rise to a unique and intriguing mythos which we will look at next.

CHAPTER 3: CREATION OF THE RUNES
-SOUND AND COSMIC ORDER-

Before we embark on this exploration, it's essential to acknowledge that significant and explicit connections between Norse creation myths and the concept of vibrational sound in ancient texts is not verifiable. The idea of sound as a fundamental force is a cornerstone in many spiritual and philosophical traditions, but its direct linkage to the Norse runes is my personal interpretation, drawing from broader Indo-European linguistic and mythological parallels. While I am not alone in this view, it's important that I am transparent with my conclusions. Despite this, the journey is intriguing. It promises to weave together strands of mythology, linguistics, and esoteric thought, creating a rich tapestry of cosmogony and insight.

VIBROACOUSTICS, THE STUDY OF SOUND WAVES AND VIBRATION

An article published in the journal, *Neuroscience & Bio-behavioral Reviews*, explains how a study on the affectionately called, 'Jedi Rats', is shedding new light on vibrational sound.

Vibroacoustics, or **ultrasonic vibrations**, suggests that the rodents are using the sound vibration of their vocalizations to cause airborne particles to form in a way that creates greater odor reception of chemical signals. Eduardo Mercado III, Ph.D., a professor of psychology in the UB College of Arts and Sciences explains how this process literally "shakes up" their physical surroundings in ways that influence how the rats inhale particles, suggesting that the sound vibrations produced enhances their sense of smell. The rodent vocalizer can then detect friends or strangers, giving an evolutionary advantage and possibly more sophisticated cognitive processes, including attention and memory. Thought and memory. Mercado says, "It almost seems like magic."

The "magic" of sound was not lost on Old Norse speakers. Practices such as galdr and vardlokkur were believed to have the power to influence events and spirits, and often used for protection, divination, or summoning. Vardlokkur is a type of spiritual magic song or charm found in Old Norse literature, particularly in the Eddas and Sagás. The word Galdr is believed to come from the Old Norse verb, "gala" meaning to scream or crow. It was a combination of chanting, rhythmic movements, song, and other vocal expressions used to manipulate sound to induce trances or altered states of consciousness.

A complex spiritual practice in Norse culture, galdr and vardlokkur are still used today as a form of magic or spellcasting. The rhythmic and repetitive aspect of galdr is believed to have a powerful effect on the mind and spirit. Understanding this potential connection between sound and runes establishes a foundation of Norse cosmology.

According to this mythology, the cosmos began with Ginnungagap, the primordial void. From this emptiness emerged two realms: Niflheim, the realm of ice, cold, and mist, and also Muspelheim, the realm of fire and heat. At their boundary, a giant, Ymir, was born. From Ymir's body, the world was formed. The gods, the Aesir, emerged from this cosmic creation. Central to the Norse worldview is the concept of order amidst chaos, a dynamic equilibrium between creation and destruction.

The runes, as we shall see, can be interpreted as symbols of this cosmic dance. Some leaning more to creation energy and some with more destructive elements. While there is no explicit Norse myth detailing the creation of the runes, their origins are often linked to Oðin, the "Allfather". In the Rúnatal, Óðin recounts his self-sacrifice. He hangs himself from the World Tree, Yggdrasil, for nine long nights, enduring immense pain and deprivation. As a reward for this extreme ordeal, Óðin is granted a glimpse into the hidden knowledge of the runes.

He learns not only their shapes but also their profound meanings and powers as seen below:

138 I know that I hung on a wind. Battered tree nine long nights , pierced by a spear and given to odin myself to myself on that tree whose roots grow in a place no one has ever seen

139 No one gave me food. No one gave me drink at the end.I peered down. I took the runes screaming I took them and then I fell.

140 I learned nine spells from the famous son of bolthór the father of besla and I won a drink of that precious mead poured from Óðrerir.

141 I began to be fruitful. I became wise.I grew and I thrived one word. Chased another word flowing from my mouth. One deed chased another deed flowing from my hands.

142 You will find runes, runic letters to read. Very great runes, very powerful runes. Which Oðin painted and which the holy gods made and which Oðin carved.

143 Óðin carved for the gods and Dáne for the elves, Dvalin for the dwarves and Ásvid for the giants; I carved some myself.
144 Do you know how to write them? Do you know how to paint them? Do you know how to ask them? Do you know how to send them? Do you know how to offer them?

145. It is better not to pray at all than to pray for too much. Nothing will be given that you won't repay. It is better to sacrifice nothing than to offer too much Óðin carved this before the birth of human kind when he rose up and returned again.

-The Hávamál; Rúnital Stanzas 138-145

Óđin is said to have hung himself from the world tree, Yggdrasil, sacrificing himself to himself, to gain knowledge of the runes. This dramatic act underscores the profound significance of the runes in Norse culture and what is required to obtain them. Before delving into the potential connection between runes and sound within the Norse context, it's helpful to examine the broader concept of sound as a creative principle.

Many ancient cultures, from the Vedic traditions of India to the Pythagorean philosophy of Greece, viewed sound as the fundamental building block of the universe. The idea of the "cosmic word" or "divine sound" is prevalent in these traditions. The concept is often linked to creation myths, suggesting that the universe emerged from a primordial vibration.

Language itself is a form of sound. It is through spoken and written language that we structure our reality, communicate our thoughts, and shape our world. The power of words is a common theme in many mythologies, and the Norse worldview is no exception.

If we consider the runes as a form of written language, and if we accept the premise that language is inherently connected to sound, then it becomes plausible to explore a link between the runes and vibration. Ymir, the first primordial giant in the Norse creation myth is our first example of Norse thought regarding sound and creation. One of the most common interpretations of the translation of Ymir's name in Old Norse means "screamer." This could allude to the chaotic and violent nature of the primordial world.

I will refer to Ymir with the pronoun "they" as they were neither male or female, or perhaps both. Ymir played a crucial role in the creation of the cosmos. As they slept, their body parts grew into various beings, including the first giants. When the gods Óđin, Vili, and Vé decided to create order from chaos, they killed Ymir and used its body to construct the world. Ymir's flesh became the earth, their bones the mountains, their blood the oceans, and their skull the sky. In essence, Ymir represents the raw, unformed potential from which the universe emerged. Emerging through the scream of chaos. Some scholars interpret the name of Ymir's sustenance giving primordial cow, Auðhumla, as "abundance of humming," suggesting another surprising connection between sound and creation in this myth. It's fascinating to think that the universe might emerge from a sonic source like the vocalizations and "screams" accompanying human birth.

The book of Genesis in the Torah, or Pentateuch as well as the Christian Bible states in chapter 1 vs:3, "God said let there be light, and there was light."

The often used magical word "Abracadabra" is believed to derive from ancient Hebrew meaning, "I will create as I speak." In the Christian New Testament, the Gospel of St. John 1:1 declares, "In the beginning was the Word, and the Word was with God, and the Word was God." These are just a few popular mythologies that connect language with creation.

Looking at the Hávamál stanza 139, Óðin says, "No one gave me food. No one gave me drink. At the end I peered down. I took the runes screaming, I took them and then I fell." The Old Norse word used here for screaming is øpandi. Most linguists translate this to mean screaming or shrieking. In modern Icelandic, our closest living language to Old Norse, øpandi means an opening. One can visualize the mouth opening wide and cavernous, allowing for the deepest primal scream to pour forth.

This prompts us to consider another concept. Through a guttural scream, Óðin drew the runes from their ethereal plane of existence—the Well of Urd, nestled at the base of Yggdrasil. These potent symbols resided in a realm beyond our own, until Óðin's primal vocalization pulled them into our dimension. The sound and vibration of his cry birthed the runes into our reality. Could it be that the runes were originally vocalizations? Sounds or even primal grunts of early man?

While there is no direct evidence in Norse texts linking the runes to specific sounds or vibrations, modern scholars and practitioners have proposed intriguing connections. Some suggest that the shapes of the runes correspond to specific vocalizations or even musical notes. Others propose that the runes represent archetypal sound patterns that underlie the structure of reality. It's important to approach these interpretations with caution. Often, they are based on speculative methodologies and personal insights rather than concrete historical evidence.

However, they offer a fascinating lens through which to view the runes and their creation mythos. The notion that voice, speech, language or sound served as the catalyst for creation is a recurring theme in ancient thought. Wisdom suggests we consider the possibility that other cultures as well as the Norse, may have shared this belief in their distant past.

The idea that the runes are connected to vibrational sound is a compelling one, even if it lacks definitive historical support. By exploring the broader context of sound as a cosmic force, the nature of language, and the symbolic power of the runes, we can construct a plausible framework for understanding this potential connection.

WHAT IS SOUND

Physics defines sound as a vibration that travels through a medium (like air, water, or solids) as a wave. These waves are caused by the movement of particles in the medium. The frequency of the wave determines the pitch of the sound, and the amplitude of the wave determines the loudness of the sound. Sound waves carry energy. When this energy interacts with matter, it can cause physical changes. For example, sound waves can shatter glass or create ripples in water. Certain objects can resonate at specific frequencies, amplifying sound waves. This principle is used in musical instruments and architectural acoustics. In many languages, the word for "sound" or "voice" is closely related to the word for "create." This suggests a deep-rooted belief in the creative power of language.

Some believe that the universe is constructed based on specific geometric patterns, and that sound vibrations can replicate these patterns, leading to creation. Quantum physics suggests that the universe is fundamentally made up of vibrations, and that consciousness can influence these vibrations, leading to the creation of reality.

We see this displayed in the beliefs of the ancients as well.

The ancient practice of "blessing" food or offering prayers was essentially an attempt to vibrationally harmonize oneself with the food's energetic vibration. The ultimate goal was to manifest a desired outcome through this alignment. Mainly being that the body would accept the food in a non disruptive way that wouldn't cause ill health.

The Egyptians used sacred sounds, or mantras, in their religious ceremonies. The sound of the human voice was believed to be a powerful tool for connecting with the divine. Ancient Greeks attributed great significance to music and the lyre, an instrument associated with the god Apollo. Pythagoras, a Greek philosopher and mathematician, explored the mathematical relationships between sound and the universe. Vedic chants and mantras are central to Hindu and Buddhist practices.

These sounds are believed to have the power to create, heal, and transform consciousness. Tibetan Buddhist monks use chanting and singing bowls to create harmonic sounds that are believed to induce deep states of meditation and healing.

While the ancient belief in the creative power of sound often resides in the realm of spirituality and philosophy, modern science does offer some intriguing parallels. Sound does, in fact, have a physical phenomenon. Objects have natural frequencies at which they vibrate most efficiently. When sound waves match these frequencies, resonance occurs, amplifying the vibrations. This principle is fundamental to acoustics and music. Cymatics is the study of visible sound patterns. It demonstrates how sound vibrations can create physical structures in matter, such as sand, water, or even flames, directly affecting our physical environment.

Other research suggests that certain sound frequencies can influence biological systems. For instance, some studies have explored the potential of sound therapy for pain management or relaxation. I've experienced this in my own practice while using bone tapping sound on clients. It's even theorized that specific sound frequencies can induce changes in brainwave patterns, potentially affecting mood, cognition, and consciousness, as brainwaves operate at different frequencies themselves.

While the connection between runes and the creation of sound remains shrouded in mystery, it's undeniable that Germanic peoples employed runes for magical purposes. This invites us to explore runes within the context of magic itself. Magic can be understood as the manipulation of energy to influence both the physical and non-physical realms. The Germanic peoples believed runes could be used to control natural forces and interact with supernatural entities. In essence, runes were used not just in the manipulation of energy, but as tools of manifestation.

CHAPTER 4: RUNES AS TOOLS OF MANIFESTATION

The concept of manifestation, often exploited by New Age mysticism, is fundamentally about shaping reality through intention. While I am aware of the dangers of New Age influence and appropriation of traditional practices, the idea of manifestation, though not called that, is far from novel. Ancient cultures, such as those of Scandinavia, possessed sophisticated methods for interacting with the unseen to influence the physical world. Runes, a core component of Norse tradition, were potent tools in this endeavor. The act of writing down an intention is a cornerstone of magical practice.

By externalizing a thought, it's believed to more readily penetrate the subconscious mind, the realm from which magic is often thought to originate. The subconscious mind, often described as the "hidden mind," holds immense potential for those practicing magic. Because the subconscious is a wellspring of creativity, often generating innovative and unexpected solutions to magical challenges, it can amplify intuitive abilities, allowing for deeper connections with the magical realm and a heightened sense of timing and energy. The subconscious is also believed to be connected to the collective unconscious, a vast reservoir of archetypal symbols and energies. Regular engagement with it can enhance psychic abilities like clairvoyance, clairaudience, and even empathy. It can be programmed to attract desired outcomes, aligning actions and thoughts with magical intentions.

This concept finds a compelling parallel in Norse mythology. The Norns, cosmic beings associated with destiny, are depicted as carving runes into the roots of the world tree, Yggdrasil. This act symbolizes the creation of reality itself, a potent metaphor for manifestation. Even the names of these Norns bear witness to the idea that runes can be used for divination. "Norn" itself is possibly linked to the Swedish verb, norna or nyrna meaning to "communicate secretly."

Without going into the editomology too deeply, these names carry insight into the purpose of these wise ones. Urðr represents fate that has happened in "the past" and Verðandi, "the present" or what is happening right now. Because what we do in the past and the present dictates what happens in the future, we can surmise a futuristic outcome, thus being given divinatory insight and even the possibility of changing it. That is what "Skuld" means: what "ought to be." We create a type of karmic "debt" with our actions. How we act out or pay that debt remains to be seen.

Óðin asking his readers in the Hávamál, "Do you know how to carve runes?" could possibly be interpreted as a deeper question about one's ability to translate inner vision into physical reality using the language of runes. Often credited as the creator of the runes, Óðin is more accurately seen as a mediator. He acted as a conduit, transferring these ancient symbols from an otherworldly plane into the realm of Midgard, our physical realm. While prevailing belief attributes Óðin with acquiring the runes, some interpretations suggest the Norns, the weavers of fate, may have already carved them into Yggdrasil. Óðin's sacrifice on the tree might have just been the key that unlocked their potential, allowing him to access and share these powerful symbols with the world.

The ancients seemed to grasp this principle intuitively. By giving form to a nebulous idea through the carving of a rune, they were, in essence, anchoring a thought into the material world. This process suggests a profound connection between the abstract and the concrete, the spiritual and the physical, as mediated through the symbolic power of the runes.

Before delving into the mechanics of rune-based manifestation, it's essential to clarify the term "magic." At its core, magic is the ability to induce change through non-ordinary means. Whether it's the völva (Old Norse seeress) manipulating fate with her vardlokkur (magic songs) or a modern practitioner visualizing desires into existence, the underlying principle remains the same: altering reality through consciousness and energy.

The Norns, enigmatic figures in Norse mythology, offer a compelling link between runes and manifestation. Often depicted as the givers & creators of our fate, the Norns, as mentioned previously, are associated with carving runes into the world tree, Yggdrasil. This act symbolizes the transformation of ethereal concepts into tangible reality, a process strikingly similar to contemporary manifestation techniques.

While our ancestors lacked scientific terminology, they intuitively understood the power of intention and focus. Carving runes reinforced desires, imprinting them on the subconscious mind. This process, combined with specific rituals and practices, created a potent formula for manifestation.

Just as the old Norns carved the runes into the base of world tree, the act of physically writing or carving an intention or rune, is believed to enhance its impact on the subconscious mind for several reasons. These acts engage multiple senses (sight, touch) when writing or carving thus reinforcing the intention. This heightened sensory input stimulates different areas of the brain, creating a deeper neural connection to the intention and causes a conscious to subconscious transfer. The process of physically forming words or shapes forces conscious attention to the intention, clarifying it.

With repeated focus, the intention is more likely to seep into the subconscious, influencing thoughts, beliefs, and behaviors. The written or carved physical object becomes a tangible representation of the intention, serving as a visual reminder. Physical connection can create a stronger emotional bond with the intention, increasing its potency. The act of writing or carving can also be seen as a ritual, signaling a commitment to those spirits or deities called upon for assistance or even to the intention itself. This ritualistic approach strengthens belief in the possibility of the manifestation. The physical act anchors the mind in the present moment, preventing the distractions so many of us face in our modern day and age. This focused state intensifies the energy and clarity of the intention.

Central to successful manifestation is the concept of surrender. By letting go of attachment to outcomes, practitioners can align themselves with a higher power or their inner wisdom. This state of consciousness, often achieved through meditative practices or ecstatic rituals like seiðr, is optimal for manifesting desires.

A petition itself, is a clear and concise statement of intent, and is another crucial element. It should be crafted with emotional intensity but detached from expectation. Rituals serve as catalysts, propelling the petition into the subconscious where it can incubate and manifest.

Ultimately, the most potent form of manifestation is to embody the desired outcome. This involves aligning one's identity with the desired reality. By acting as if the desired state already exists, individuals can influence their subconscious and external circumstances to match their inner vision.

Incorporating rune work into this process can amplify the effect. Each rune carries specific energies and meanings, which can be harnessed to support the manifestation process. By understanding the runes and their associations, which we will see in future chapters, practitioners can create powerful tools for transformation. Runes offer a profound pathway to manifestation. By combining ancient wisdom with contemporary understanding, individuals can tap into the power of their subconscious and shape their reality with their desires. We can see examples of this in the Poetic Edda. In the poem Sigrdrífumál, the Valkyrie Sigrdrífa shares her knowledge of runes with the hero Sigurd. She details various types of runes, including victory runes, ale runes, birth runes, and more. Each mention corresponds with a specific intention:

- Victory runes: To ensure success in battle.
- Ale runes: To protect against poisoning.
- Birth runes: To aid in childbirth.
- Wave runes: To calm the sea.
- Branch runes: For healing.
- Speech runes: To protect against verbal attacks.
- Thought runes: To enhance mental clarity.

While these runes are described for specific purposes, a broader understanding of runes as tools for influencing events is implied. The Prose Edda's Gylfaginning by Snorri Sturluson, establishes the runes as possessing magical and prophetic qualities, with the acquisition of rune knowledge central to this idea. In Egil's Saga, we find a young woman falls gravely ill. Upon investigation, Egil discovers the root of her affliction: a whalebone inscribed with runes, hidden beneath her bed.

A lovesick suitor, in a misguided attempt to win her heart, had carved these symbols with the intention of awakening her love. However, his knowledge of runes proved inadequate with his ignorance, resulting in a malevolent spell that caused the woman's illness. Egil, recognizing the danger, removed the harmful runes and destroyed the whalebone. He then crafted new runes, imbued with healing intent, and placed them beneath the woman's pillow. Gradually, her health began to mend.

Egil then gives us a cautionary note:

Runes none should grave ever
Who knows not to read them;
Of dark spell full many
The meaning may miss.
Ten spell-words writ wrongly
On whale-bone were graven:
Whence to leek-tending maiden,
Long sorrow and pain.
-Egil's Saga Chpt. 72

The previous examples all illustrate the idea and concept that Old Norse speakers truly believed that inscribed runes can manifest as an outcome in our physical realm. While not literary texts, even runestones themselves often include cryptic messages or invocations, suggesting a deeper, perhaps ritualistic, connection to the runes. Therefore we conclude that runes can act as conduits for energy, channeling it towards the desired outcome. They can be used in combination with meditation, visualization, and other magical techniques to enhance the manifestation process just as they did for the ancients who came before us.

CHAPTER 5: RUNES AS SPIRITS AND ENTITIES OF NATURE

Old Norse speakers held a profound connection to the natural world, and their belief system was deeply intertwined with it. Runes, as fundamental elements of their culture, were not merely tools of manifestation, symbols or letters but were considered to be living entities with inherent power and spirit.

The Norse accepted that the universe was a living organism, with everything interconnected. Runes were seen as microcosms of this cosmic order, representing the forces and energies that shaped the world. Each rune was often associated with a specific natural element, such as fire, water, earth, or air. This connection imbued the runes with the qualities and power of the element they represented. Some runes were linked to specific Norse gods or mythical creatures, reinforcing their spiritual significance. For instance, the rune Thurisaz was often associated with Thor, the god of thunder and the Jotnar, giants of the mythos.

Perceiving runes as possessing a life of their own, magic practitioners of runes believed them to have consciousness and the ability to interact with humans. Runes were considered a source of magical and spiritual power. By understanding and building relationships with the runes, individuals could harness these energies for various purposes, such as divination, healing, protection, and even warfare. These spirits were seen as a means of communication with the gods and other spiritual entities. Through the interpretation of rune casts, people sought guidance, wisdom, and insight.

Runes were incorporated into poetic compositions, where their sounds, vibrational energy and meanings contributed to the overall power and significance of the verse. To those attuned to the subtle energies of the world, runes became a living "alphabet", each rune connecting to the very essence of nature. More than simple representations of sounds; they were and are windows into the soul of the world, doorways to interact with the elemental forces that shape our reality. To perceive the runes as spirits is to shift one's perspective. It is to see the world not as a collection of inanimate objects, but as a vibrant tapestry of consciousness. Each rune being a conscious entity, a being of light and energy with its own unique qualities and purpose. They are the architects of creation, the guardians of the natural order. The concept of runes as spirits is deeply rooted in the animistic worldview of our ancestors.

They believed that everything in the world, from the smallest blade of grass to the mightiest oak, possessed a spirit. This animistic perspective offered a profound reverence for nature and a deep understanding of the interconnectedness of all things. Runes, as the embodiment of the natural world, reflect this animistic worldview. Uruz, the aurochs, represents primal strength and wild energy. Sowilo, rune of the sun, constitutes a life giving force & success. To work with the runes as spirits is to engage in a sacred dialogue. It is to listen to their wisdom, to seek their guidance, and to align one's own energy with their purpose.

Yes, this can be done through meditation & divination. However, what I most recommend to my students and clients, is to spend time in nature. Observing the natural rhythms in nature and feeling its subtle vibrational energy has no comparison to any other form of connection. It will change you and your relationship to the runes and their consciousness. By understanding the runes as spirits, we begin to see the world with new eyes. We recognize the patterns and frequencies of nature, the interconnectedness of all life. We develop a deeper appreciation for the beauty and complexity of the world around us, and we learn to live in harmony with the natural world.

When our perceptions start to shift, we begin to see these energies with much more respect. We acknowledge that the rune itself begins to be considered a physical manifestation of its spirit similar to an icon or statuary. It's a home for the spirit it represents to dwell and be able to interact with humans. Some practitioners believe that runes can become personal spirit guides. Through meditation and connection, they believe a person can develop a relationship with a particular rune. That rune is then seen as a source of guidance, protection, or inspiration. While we have no definitive evidence of this being a belief in Norse culture, it bares mentioning. Again, While Old Norse texts and rune poems themselves don't explicitly refer to runes as spirits or conscious entities, there's a rich tapestry of interpretation and belief that has developed around them. Over time, the concept of runes as spiritual beings has become more pronounced.

However, when we consider the broader context of Norse and Germanic cultures, and examine that these societies held animistic beliefs, attributing spirits and souls to natural objects and phenomena, it is plausible that how they perceived runes was influenced by this worldview. Let's explore the benefits of how this point of view can enhance a practitioner's experience with rune casting. The practice of rune casting, a divination method commonly associated with Norse culture, offers a profound connection to the past and a gateway to deeper spiritual understanding.

When runes are viewed as spiritual entities, it is believed they are then capable of enhancing the divinatory process and providing rich insights beyond surface interpretations. Norse mythology saturates runes with a sacred aura. By perceiving runes as living entities, the runecaster establishes a more intimate relationship with these symbols, allowing for a deeper resonance with their inherent energies. When runes are viewed as spiritual beings, the casting becomes a form of communication rather than a mere random selection. The runecaster invites these entities to participate in the process, seeking their guidance and perspective. This approach fosters a more intuitive and personal connection to the runes, enabling the diviner to tap into deeper layers of meaning. Runes may reveal not only external circumstances but also internal states, offering a holistic understanding of the situation.

Furthermore, treating runes as spiritual entities can enhance the divinatory experience by promoting a heightened state of consciousness. As the runecaster engages with the runes on a spiritual level, they may experience a shift in perception, allowing for greater clarity and insight. This expanded awareness can facilitate a deeper connection with the underlying energies at play, enabling the diviner to discern patterns and underlying truths that may have been obscured. The relationship between the runecaster and the runes is a dynamic one. Through consistent practice and building this connection, the diviner can cultivate a deeper understanding of each rune's unique qualities.

This intimate knowledge allows for more nuanced interpretations and a greater ability to discern the subtleties of a casting. Over time, the runes may even reveal personal messages or guidance, forming a unique and evolving relationship. Incorporating the concept of runes as spiritual entities into a rune casting practice can significantly deepen the divinatory experience. By fostering a more profound bond with these ancient characters, the runecaster opens themselves to a wealth of wisdom and insight. This approach transforms rune casting from a mechanical process into a sacred ritual, inviting a deeper exploration of self and the world around us.

In the chapters to follow, we will delve deeper into the individual runes, exploring their meanings, correspondences, and the ways in which they manifest as spirits in the natural world.

CHAPTER 6: RUNE MEANINGS AND ÆTTS

While the enigmatic Elder Futhark, the earliest known Germanic alphabet, undoubtedly possessed a rich nomenclature for its twenty-four runes, the exact nature of these original names remains recessed in the mists of time. Though likely removed from their original names, Scholars and linguists alike agree that these ancient designations in all likelihood have evolved into the rune names familiar to us today. Unlike the abstract symbols of many writing systems, runes are multifaceted, serving as both visual and phonetic representations. This multiplicity is evident in the modern rune names, which often begin with the sound the rune signifies.

For instance, the "m" rune is called mannaz, meaning "man" or "human being," while the "h" rune is known as hagalaz, signifying "hail." This interconnectedness of sound and meaning underscores the holistic approach of the runic script. It is crucial to note that our definitive knowledge of rune names primarily stems from the Viking Age. The eight runes absent from the Viking Age Younger Futhark have been reconstructed through careful comparison with the Anglo-Saxon runic alphabet. While this process offers valuable insights, it is essential to acknowledge the limitations of such reconstructions in fully capturing the essence of the original Elder Futhark and its categorizations.

The pervasive misconceptions surrounding runes and divination in recent times cannot be overemphasized. While acknowledging the historical inaccuracies that have flourished, it's equally important to recognize the contemporary practice of rune divination. Despite its association with dubious historical roots, the use of runes for predictive purposes has become widespread.

Contrary to popular belief, there's no evidence of a structured, ancient system for rune divination. The esoteric application of runes was shrouded in secrecy throughout antiquity, leaving us with scant historical records. Armed with this knowledge, we can approach the runes with a critical yet open mind. By recognizing their potential for contemporary use without relying on unfounded historical claims, we can explore the possibility of tapping into the inherent power of these symbols for modern-day guidance.

Traditionally, the Elder Futhark is divided into three groups of eight runes, called ætts, families or clans. This structure is believed to reflect the Germanic worldview, which we know was deeply connected to nature and its rhythms. The division into three ætts, mirrors the cyclical nature of life as understood by the Norse speaking peoples. Many believe that the ætts possible origins spring from their alignment with the concept of the three realms in Norse mythology: Ásgarðr (home of the gods), Midgard (the world of humans), and Helheimr or Hel (the underworld of the dead).

Johannes Bureus (1658-1652), the great Swedish polymath, mystic and antiquarian, was a significant figure in the study and interpretation of runes that we know today. He traversed the Scandinavian countryside, recording oral histories with elderly farmers and practitioners of folk customs. His research focused on documenting traditional rune usage.

While Bureus is attributed to much insight, the concept of dividing the alphabet into groups or sets of eight, predates him. This idea likely has its roots in the oral traditions and poetic structures of Northern European cultures. It's possible that these divisions were based on mythological, cosmological, or practical considerations. The number eight held symbolic importance for Bureus. It represented infinity, cycles, and completion. Dividing the runes into three groups of eight reinforced his concept of a cyclical and interconnected universe. Bureus' contribution lies in his systematization of these divisions and his extensive work on runelore, which greatly influenced later scholars.

THE THREE ÆTTS:

Often associated with different aspects of life, the cosmos, or the human experience.

Freyr's Ætt: Named after Freyr, a Norse fertility god, this ætt is associated with beginnings, growth, and the spring season. Themes of creation, birth and the ascending aspect of existence dominate this ætt. It represents the beginning of life and the waking of nature. Often connecting to themes of love, prosperity and reproduction. The runes in this ætt can represent sounds associated with the beginning of words. Freyr's Ætt is akin to the creation of the world, the forces within us, and the growth of life. The runes within this ætt are: Fehu, Uruz, Thurisaz, Ansuz, Raido, Kaunan, Gebo and Wunjo.

Hagalaz Ætt: Named after Hagalaz, a rune often associated with hail or storm, this ætt represents change, chaos, and winter. Linked to the middle stages of life, whether ordered or disordered, it often connects to themes of conflict, change, and inner strength. Seen as a transitional period between maturation and harvest, Hagalaz Ætt symbolizes the external forces and challenges of life, mirroring the chaotic nature of Midgard. Runes Hagalaz, Nauthiz, Isa, Year, Eihwaz, Perthro, Algiz and Sowilo comprise Hagal's ætt.

Tyr's Ætt: Named after Tyr, the Norse god of war, law, and self sacrifice, this ætt symbolizes harvest, completion, and the end of the cycle. Representing wisdom, destiny, and the evolution of transformation. It joins themes of law, order, and spiritual growth. The runes here can represent sounds at the end of words. Tyr's Ætt encompasses the end of a cycle, similar to the concept of death and the afterlife in Helheimr. This ætt symbolizes the descending and transformative process and consists of runes Tiwaz,Berkana, Ehwaz, Mannaz, Laguz, Ingwaz, Dagaz and Othala.

Next, we'll delve into the individual meanings of the twenty-four Elder Futhark runes. Each interpretation is a synthesis of historical knowledge, contemporary comprehension, and my personal insights and observations to create a cohesive understanding. To avoid confusion, I will also be using the Proto-Germanic spellings associated with the elder futhark runes.

Fehu: Rune Of Cattle, Wealth, And Abundance

Fehu represents the fundamental forces of abundance, life, and beginnings. Linked to the Old English word "feoh," meaning cattle or wealth, it etymologically puts Fehu in a more literal light. However, in the context of the rune, wealth is not merely material possessions but can encompass a broader spectrum, including various kinds of abundance and prosperity. In modern times, it signifies the wealth that flows through life, not just in terms of material goods, but also in the richness of experiences and relationships. The rune's association with cattle also carries symbolic weight. Cattle were essential to the livelihood of pre-Christian Scandinavian peoples, providing food, clothing, and a means of exchange. In this sense, Fehu represents the foundation of sustenance, the basic necessities of life. It is a reminder of the importance of grounding oneself, of building a solid base from which to grow and expand. As the first rune of the Futhark, lore has Fehu is associated with the Norse god Freyja, a deity of fertility, abundance, and prosperity. These connections deepen the rune's symbolism, linking it to themes of creation, growth, and the cycles of nature. It is the seed from which all growth emerges. This rune encourages initiative and enterprise, urging the individual to embrace new opportunities and ventures. For many, Fehu is deeply connected to the concept of personal power. It represents the ability to create one's own reality, to manifest desires, and to harness the energy of the universe. A rune of immense power and potential. It embodies the fundamental principles of life: creation, growth, and abundance. By understanding the essence of Fehu, individuals can tap into its energy to create an understanding of life of prosperity and purpose.

Uruz: Rune Of Raw, Primal Power

Derived from the Old Norse word "auroux," meaning wild ox or auroch, Uruz embodies the strength, vitality, and endurance of this formidable creature. It is a symbol of primal energy, representing the force that drives creation and sustains life. Like the auroch, Uruz signifies a powerful, independent spirit, a refusal to be subdued or controlled. At its core, Uruz is a rune of transformation. It signifies the potential for great change, often abrupt and unexpected. This change is not necessarily gentle or easy; it can be as forceful as the auroch charging through a forest. Yet, it is ultimately a positive force, leading to growth and renewal.

Uruz encourages us to tap into our inner strength and will power to overcome obstacles, and to embrace challenges as opportunities for personal evolution. It suggests that a situation demands strength, courage, and decisiveness. However, it is essential to channel this energy wisely. Uruz can also warn of potential aggression or recklessness if not balanced with wisdom and control. Inversely, depending on its placement, it can even imply physical weakness or illness. Beyond its association with physical strength, Uruz also speaks to inner fortitude. It represents the ability to withstand adversity, to persevere through challenges, and to emerge stronger on the other side. This rune can be a source of inspiration for those facing difficult times, reminding us of our own resilience and capacity for overcoming obstacles.

Thurisaz: Thorns And Giants

The Thurisaz rune is a symbol steeped in potent and paradoxical energies. Often perceived with a degree of caution, it is a rune that demands respect and understanding. Its name translates to "thorn" or "giant, ogre" both of which offer profound insights into its multifaceted nature. Like mjölnir, the beloved hammer of the God Thor, Thurisaz represents raw, unfiltered power. It is the force of nature, both destructive and creatively protective. Like a thorn, it can cause pain and injury, yet it also serves as a protective barrier. It is the force of resistance, the immovable object that stands against overwhelming pressure.

In this sense, Thurisaz is a symbol of courage and resilience. It is the strength to confront adversity, to stand one's ground, and to persevere. Giants, or Jötnar, while often portrayed as chaotic, destructive forces, were also fundamental to the cosmic order. They represented the wild, untamed aspects of existence, the forces that must be both feared and respected. Thurisaz, which many associate with giants, therefore, embodies the wildness within us, the untamed spirit that seeks expression.

It is a call to connect with our inner power, to embrace our primal nature, and to use it wisely. Just as a thorn can pierce the skin to allow for healing, so too can Thurisaz provoke change. It can disrupt the status quo, forcing us to confront our fears and limitations. It is a catalyst for growth, urging us to break free from old patterns and embrace new possibilities. While protective, its effect is not always comfortable. The key to interpreting Thurisaz lies in understanding its dual nature. It is a reminder of our own inner power, the capacity for both, destruction and creation. It is a call to embrace the wildness within us, to confront our fears, and to emerge stronger on the other side. In the brokenness, a level plain is cleared for new growth to emerge.

Ansuz: The God Rune

Ansuz is often etymologically linked to the Old Norse word for mouth, symbolizing the power of the spoken word and the mouth of the divine. Many refer to this rune as the rune of the high one, Óđin and his önd (breath). As the god of wisdom, poetry, and magic, Óđin is believed to have sacrificed an eye to drink from the Well of Mimir, gaining the ability to perceive the hidden truths of the cosmos and deep, profound knowledge. Ansuz encourages effective communication, emphasizing the importance of clear expression and active listening as well as signifying the arrival of important messages or insights from the divine. Ansuz can also warn against careless speech or the misuse of language. The rune serves as a reminder of the potential consequences of our words and the responsibility we bear in shaping reality through our communication.

In a deeper spiritual context, Ansuz represents the connection between the human and divine realms. It suggests that inspiration and guidance can be found through meditation, prayer, or other forms of spiritual practice and listening. By tuning into the inner voice, individuals can access a wellspring of wisdom and creativity. It invites us to embrace the power of communication, to seek knowledge with an open mind, and to use our words wisely and intentionally. By understanding the deeper meaning of this rune, we can harness its energy to enhance our lives and connect more deeply with the world around us. Ansuz confirms and reminds us of the sacred nature of language and the profound impact it can have on our lives and the lives of others. It has the ability to encourage us to use our voices for good, to spread love, compassion, and understanding, and to create a world that is harmonious and just.

Raido: Journey's Path

Raido is believed to derive from the Proto-Germanic root *reid-, signifying "ride," "journey" or "carriage." Often it's viewed as a signal to inform the reader of a physical move or travel ahead. From a spiritual perspective, this core meaning extends far beyond mere physical travel. The rune encapsulates the idea of progress, movement, and the dynamic nature of existence. It is a symbol of the path, be it the road ahead, the course of life, or the inner exploration of the self. Raido signifies forward motion, progress, and success. It is a sign of good fortune, indicating that one is on the right path. It can represent a journey that is both physically and spiritually rewarding. The rune encourages the seeker to embrace change and to view challenges and growth as cyclical patterns in nature. It is a reminder that life is a continuous journey, and that it is essential to maintain a sense of direction and purpose. Raido can also signify delays, obstacles, or detours. It may indicate that one is on the wrong path or that it is time to reassess one's goals depending on its placement in a cast. Yet, even in this context, the rune does not imply failure or defeat. Instead, it suggests a need for patience, perseverance, and adaptability. It is a call to trust the process and to find new paths when necessary.

It encapsulates the dynamic nature of life, the importance of journey, and the need for both forward motion and adaptability. It is also deeply connected to the concept of destiny. Suggesting that our lives are shaped by the choices we make, but also by forces beyond our control. The journey, therefore, is not merely about reaching a destination, but about the experiences and growth that occur along the way.

Kenaz/Kaunan:Rune Of Illumination

Kaunan is the Proto-Germanic name for the rune that represents the sound "k". While it directly translates to "ulcer" or "sore" in Old Norse, its symbolic meaning could possibly be more complex and multifaceted. Another interpretation is the assigned name Kenaz, which is the Anglo-Saxon designation for the same rune representing the consonant "k."

Whether a torch, flame, ulcer or wound, there's an argument that Kaunan/Kenaz seems to be associated with burning. This representation is central to its contemporary meaning. Like fire, Kenaz/Kaunan can be both constructive and destructive. While it brings light and warmth, it can also consume and purify. This duality reflects the challenges of personal growth. The transformative power of this rune can lead to profound change, but it also requires courage and resilience. Just as a torch dispels darkness, Kenaz signifies the illumination of the mind. It is a rune associated with inspiration, insight, and the acquisition of knowledge.

The flame of Kenaz ignites curiosity, encouraging exploration and the pursuit of understanding. It is the spark that ignites creativity, fueling artistic endeavors and innovative thought. Beyond intellectual illumination, this rune with multiple designations also embodies a spiritual dimension. It represents the inner light, the soul's capacity for self-discovery and growth. In this sense, it is a beacon, guiding one through the complexities of existence and the development of wisdom. It may indicate the emergence of new ideas or the development of creative projects. However, it can also warn of potential challenges or the need to confront hidden wounds, or negative aspects of oneself. The interpretation of Kenaz/Kaunan is dependent on the surrounding runes and the specific context of the reading.

Gebo: Gift And Exchange

The shape of Gebo itself is evocative of its meaning. Two triangular forms intertwine, creating a symmetrical and balanced image. This visual representation reinforces the idea of partnership and equality. It suggests that in every exchange, both parties are enriched. There is no hierarchy, no dominance. Instead, there is a mutual respect and understanding. Equilibrium is paramount in any dynamic relationship. Reciprocity becomes an imperative; what one party willingly offers necessitates a corresponding action from the recipient.

Gebo embodies the spirit of gift, generosity and mutual exchange. Beyond the personal level, Gebo also speaks to the larger cosmic order. It embodies the consummation of sexual energy, mirroring the rhythmic patterns of life itself. Just as the seasons ebb and flow, exchanging vitalities, the universe manifests its cosmic dance.

By giving freely, we contribute to the overall balance of the world. In a divinatory context, Gebo often signifies partnerships, collaborations and even marriage. It can also indicate a time of abundance, generosity, and reciprocity.

Wunjo: Rune Of Joy

Meaning "joy" in its Proto-Germanic form, Wunjo is not merely a fleeting happiness but but a profound sense of well-being that arises from a harmonious connection to oneself and the world. The rune encourages us to cultivate gratitude and appreciation for life's blessings, to find joy in the simple things, and to embrace the beauty that surrounds us. Wunjo offers a powerful reminder of the importance of joy in our lives. It invites us to seek out moments of happiness in the mundane, to cultivate a positive outlook, and to embrace the fullness of life. In a world often filled with challenges and uncertainties, Wunjo stands as a beacon of hope, inspiring us to find joy even in the midst of adversity. It indicates the realization of hopes and dreams, a sense of purpose, and a deep connection to one's true self. Wunjo may also suggest the need to celebrate achievements, to share joy with others, or to create a more joyful environment. Ultimately, contentment is an internal compass, guiding one to inner peace, happiness and lasting joy.

Hagalaz: The Hailstorm

Hagalaz, in Old Norse, directly translates to "hail" and is a symbol of powerful, disruptive change. Often associated with chaos, its image evokes a sudden, forceful, and often destructive force of nature. Yet, like a tempest that clears the air, Hagalaz signifies a necessary upheaval, paving the way for renewal and growth. At its core, Hagalaz represents the uncontrollable forces that shape our lives. It is a reminder that we are not always in control of our circumstances. Often signaling past, present or future trauma, it alerts the reader to where a crisis could arise from, thus giving possible opportunities to avoid such conflicts. It may herald job loss, relationship breakdowns, or unexpected life events.

While these experiences can be painful, they are also opportunities for profound transformation. Just as hail can damage crops but also fertilize the soil, Hagalaz suggests that even destructive forces can bring about positive change. It encourages us to embrace adversity, to find strength in vulnerability, and to trust in the process of transformation. By surrendering to the storm, we can discover hidden reserves of resilience and emerge from the chaos stronger than before.

Hagalaz is a potent reminder that change is inevitable and often necessary. It invites us to approach life with a spirit of adaptability and courage. By understanding the transformative power of Hagalaz, we can navigate life's storms with greater wisdom and resilience, ultimately emerging stronger and more connected to our true selves and those around us. While Hagalaz can be a challenging rune to encounter, it is also a deeply empowering one. It offers the promise of rebirth and renewal, inviting us to embrace the unknown with curiosity and hope.

Naudiz: Need Fire

This reconstructed Proto-Germanic name derived from Old Norse, Naudiz translates to "need" or "distress," immediately setting the tone for its complex meaning. It symbolizes resistance and friction that can take place to cause the spark needed for illumination. Often unjustly feared in readings, it represents the trials and tribulations that life inevitably presents. It is a stark reminder that hardship is an inherent part of the human experience and that growth can only come from struggle.

As the laws of physics dictate within the cosmos, friction, the resistance to motion, is the essential catalyst for ignition. From this crucible of opposition emerges the spark and flame, a testament to the transformative power of adversity. Whether it be financial difficulties, personal loss, or physical ailment, Nauthiz acknowledges the harsh realities that can test one's fortitude. It is meant to give us hope that these challenges are not meant to defeat us but encourages us to tap into our inner strength, to find the courage to endure, and to discover the resources within ourselves to overcome adversity.

Alluding to the crossed wooden sticks of the sacred need fire, so desired by these circumpolar people, Naudiz's spark can only be born from life's challenges with persistence, strength & resilience.

Isa:Rune of Ice And Stillness

Often translated as "ice", Isa encapsulates the essence of stillness, pause, and introspection. Like the icy grip of winter, Isa represents a period of stagnation, a time when outward action is halted, and inward exploration becomes paramount.

Isa signifies a necessary period of reflection. It's a call to slow down, to disconnect from the external world, and to turn one's attention inward. This internal journey can be uncomfortable, as it often involves confronting hidden fears, doubts, unresolved issues or blockages. Similar to how ice can be both destructive and constructive, healing or harmful, the Isa rune carries both challenges and opportunities. As ice preserves life beneath its frozen surface, this rune suggests that even in the midst of stillness, growth and transformation are occurring. Isa represents a necessary pause in the cycle of life, a time for introspection, and the potential for growth and transformation.

However, much like ice, which initially soothes and anesthetizes an injury, prolonged exposure can hinder the healing process. Similarly, while the introspective energy of Isa offers temporary respite, extended dwelling within its depths can impede personal growth and development. By embracing the stillness and challenges associated with this rune, individuals can emerge from the experience stronger, wiser, and better equipped to navigate life's journey.

Jera: Rune Of Harvest And Cycles

Jera's name derives from the Old Norse word for "good fruitful year," reflecting its base meaning of the cyclical nature of time and the world. The image of Jera often evokes the agricultural cycle, from sowing seeds to harvesting crops. This metaphor extends to all areas of life, suggesting that consistent effort and perseverance will eventually lead to desired outcomes. However, Jera also implies that this process takes time and cannot be rushed. It encourages patience and trust in the natural order of things.

At its heart, Jera represents the concept of reaping what you sow. It signifies a period of fruition and abundance, where the efforts and seeds planted in the past bear fruit. This rune is not merely about material gain, but also encompasses spiritual growth and the culmination of personal journeys. A time stamp rune, with implications of the cyclical year, Jera also symbolizes spiritual growth and harvest. It can represent the culmination of a personal journey, a deeper understanding of oneself, or a connection to something greater.

Eihwaz: Yew Tree Of Transformation

Deeply connected to the concept of transformation and endurance and associated with the yew tree, it symbolizes the link to burial grounds and the journey between life and death. It signifies profound change and endurance. Like the yew tree, it embodies resilience and strength in adversity. There are references to the strong roots of the tree of Yggdrasil in this rune as well. As mentioned, Eihwaz is a potent symbol of transformation. This doesn't just mean external changes; it often indicates a profound internal shift.

Just as transformation can be uncomfortable, so can this rune. However soon discomfort and intense vulnerability give way to a higher plane of existence. Eihwaz might appear as a sign of significant transformation or a necessary challenge on the horizon. It could indicate a period of intense growth or a need for strong boundaries. The rune may also suggest a deep-seated strength that will be required to navigate upcoming trials. Ultimately, Eihwaz offers a message of resilience and the promise of renewal following a period of transformation.

Perthro: Rune Of Mystery

Perthro remains a mystifying rune, cloaked in uncertainty regarding its original meaning. While some scholars propose a connection to the Old English "peord," signifying "lot" or "game," this interpretation is far from conclusive. The rune's true essence continues to elude definitive comprehension.

Perthro, to me, embodies the concept of fate. In my tradition, it's believed that the Norns weave an intricate tapestry for each individual at birth. This tapestry outlines a path, a blend of predetermined events and choices that shape our destiny.

It Is a reminder that not everything is within our control, and that embracing the unknown can lead to unexpected opportunities. This interpretation aligns with the rune's association with secrets, intuition, and the subconscious mind. It encourages us to delve into the depths of our being, to uncover hidden truths and tap into our inner wisdom. Perthro is linked to feminine energy, creativity, and fertility. It is seen as a symbol of the cyclical nature of life, death, and rebirth.

The rune represents the power of creation and the potential for new life to emerge from the depths of the obscure. While the exact meaning of Perthro has been debated by scholars for centuries, its enigmatic nature is part of its allure. It invites personal interpretation and exploration. For some, it is a symbol of hope and possibility, while for others, it represents a call to surrender to the unknown.

Algiz: Stag Of Protection

Often translated as "elk, moose" the evolution of its meaning is far more profound: protection. While the exact origins of the rune's name and form are subject to debate, its core meaning of protection remains consistent across various interpretations.

This rune carries a potent energy shield, symbolizing safety, guidance, and spiritual connection.

The image of the elk, with its powerful antlers, is a fitting representation of Algiz. Just as the elk uses its antlers for defense, this rune offers a shield against life's challenges. It signifies the ability to stand strong in the face of adversity, drawing upon inner resources for resilience. Beyond physical protection, Algiz is deeply connected to the spiritual realm. It represents a bridge between the human world and the divine, symbolizing a connection to higher powers. Divine protection.

This rune encourages individuals to trust in a greater plan and seek guidance from intuition and spiritual wisdom. Generally considered a positive omen, whether one interprets Algaz' imagery as the foot of a crow or a stag's antlers. It suggests that there is under divine protection afoot and that obstacles can be overcome with strength, determination and possible divine interference. This rune empowers individuals to face difficulties with courage and an element of faith. Whether seen as a symbol of physical defense, spiritual guidance, Algiz is a potent symbol of protection and solace, revered for centuries as a talisman against adversity.

Sowilo: Rune Of The Sun

The Sowilo rune is intimately connected to the sun. Its name itself translates to sól in Old Norse or "sun" in Proto-Germanic, underscoring its solar essence. As a representation of life giving energy and the indomitable human spirit, Sowilo embodies the sun's vital role in sustaining life on Earth. To a circumpolar people who often went without the sun's presence during winter months, It symbolized warmth, light, growth, and sustenance. Essential elements for both physical and spiritual development.

In the frigid expanse of Northern Europe, the sun was an indispensable benefactor, a celestial architect of life. Its radiant warmth was more than a mere source of heat; it was a vital catalyst, nurturing the very essence of existence in a land often gripped by winter's icy dominion. Recognizing its profound impact, these early peoples elevated the sun beyond a cosmic body, endowing it with divine attributes centered on its worship.

Just as the sun illuminated their world, dispelling darkness, Sowilo represents clarity, insight, and the ability to see through illusions. It is a beacon of hope, offering guidance and direction during challenging times. This rune is often associated with success, personal power, leadership, and the ability to manifest one's desires. It is a reminder that within each of us resides an inner light capable of overcoming adversity. It can represent the soul's journey towards enlightenment and the integration of light into one's being. Historically, the Sowilo rune held significant importance for various Germanic peoples. It was often incorporated into protective amulets and talismans, believed to ward off evil and bring good fortune. Sailors, in particular, revered Sowilo as a guiding star, helping them navigate treacherous waters. In modern times, the Sowilo rune continues to resonate with people seeking personal growth, healing, and empowerment.

Tiwaz: Justice and sacrifice

The Norse deity Tyr, is a figure of immense respect in Norse mythology. He is often depicted as a one-handed god, a testament to his ultimate act of bravery and sacrifice. In a testament to unparalleled courage, Tyr, the Norse god of war, offered his hand as a pledge of good faith to the monstrous wolf Fenrir. Aware of the impending cataclysm should the beast remain unbound, Tyr's sacrifice was a calculated act of heroism and bravery. When the gods betrayed their promise, Fenrir's jaws clamped shut, claiming Tyr's hand. This ultimate act of selfless devotion ensured the wolf's confinement, safeguarding the cosmos from imminent destruction.

Tiwaz, the rune of Tyr, reflecting this mythic archetype, is a potent symbol of valor. It signifies the courage to face one's fears, to stand up for what is right, and to make sacrifices for the greater good. This rune is not merely about physical bravery, but also about inner strength and moral fortitude. It represents the warrior spirit, the determination to overcome obstacles, and the resilience to endure hardship for sacrifice. The rune can also point to the importance of honor, integrity, and upholding one's just values.

Tiwaz also encapsulates the concept of justice and law. As the god of law, Tyr represents order and fairness. The rune can therefore suggest the need for balance and impartiality, or indicate a situation where justice needs to be upheld or where there is a disturbance of justice.

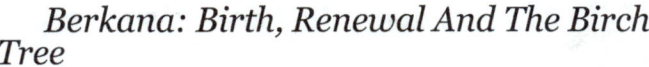

Berkana: Birth, Renewal And The Birch Tree

The name Berkana derives from the birch tree, a hardy and resilient species that is often one of the first to emerge after the harshness of winter. This association perfectly encapsulates the essence of Berkana. Berkana represents the feminine principle, embodying nurturing, creativity, and the cyclical nature of existence and birth. It is a rune deeply connected to the goddess archetype, symbolizing the mother, the healer, and the midwife. Just as the birch tree gives birth to new life each spring, Berkana signifies the power of creation and the potential for new beginnings. This rune is often associated with pregnancy, childbirth, and motherhood, but its meaning extends far beyond these physical manifestations. It encompasses the process of inner growth, personal development, and the cultivation of one's potential and ideas.

Berkana encourages us to tap into our own nurturing qualities and to create a supportive environment for ourselves and others. Not solely about beginnings, it also acknowledges the end of cycles and the inevitability of change. The birch tree, while a symbol of rebirth, also sheds its bark, signifying the letting go of the old to make way for the new. In this sense, Berkana can represent endings, loss, and the courage to embrace transformation. The rune's flexibility and resilience, like the birch tree, serve as a powerful metaphor for hope while adapting to change. It is a reminder that even in the face of adversity, there is always the potential for growth and renewal.

Ehwaz: Partnership

Ehwaz, "horse" in Old Norse, was an indispensable cornerstone of Norse existence, revered as both a precious commodity and a loyal companion. These magnificent creatures served as the lifeblood of their society. They were a precious commodity, a form of transportation, and their martial prowess. As such, the Ehwaz rune encapsulates the profound and multifaceted bond between humanity and equine, a partnership that was as essential as it was revered. A metaphor for dynamic partnerships, Ehwaz represents trust, loyalty as well as movement forward.

The relationship between a horse and rider is one of profound interdependence, requiring mutual respect and cooperation. Whether a romantic relationship, a business alliance, or even a spiritual connection, Ehwaz can encompass this bond. The horse is also a symbol of transportation, progress and journey. In both its literal and metaphorical interpretations, Ehwaz provides valuable guidance on relationships, personal growth, and life's ongoing journey.

Mannaz: Man

Deriving from the Proto-Germanic word for "man," Mannaz encapsulates humanity, community, and cooperation. It promotes the individual's responsibility within one's community. The modern Nordic model prioritizes equality in all areas. Scandinavian societies are renowned for their emphasis on collective well-being over individual achievement, something that is a foreign concept in many other countries.

While Mannaz can refer to the individual, its broader significance lies in our interconnectedness and collective potential. It represents the essence of being human. It acknowledges our strengths, weaknesses, and the complexities of our nature. The rune encourages self-awareness and personal growth, reminding us of our potential for both great deeds and mistakes. It is a call to embrace our individuality while recognizing our shared humanity and need for one another.

Beyond the individual, Mannaz signifies the importance of community and cooperation. It reflects the understanding that we are social creatures who thrive through mutual support and shared goals. The rune promotes harmony, empathy, and a sense of belonging. It reminds us of our responsibility to contribute positively to the collective well-being. It can also indicate the importance of relationships, teamwork, and cooperation in achieving goals. Essentially, Mannaz is a reminder of our shared human experience and the importance of both individual and collective development.

Laguz: Water

Embodying the element of water Laguz, "water" or "lake" in Proto-Germanic, encapsulates the fluidity, depth, and transformative power associated with its namesake. Laguz represents the flow of life. Like water, it signifies constant movement, change, flexibility and adaptation. Water is a symbol of the subconscious mind, as well as emotion. This rune invites us to delve into the watery world of our inner selves. It represents intuition, dreams, and emotions, suggesting a need for introspection and self-awareness.

Growing up in my home town of Niagara Falls, amidst the thundering majesty of the cataracts, I developed a profound respect for water as an elemental force, witnessing firsthand the colossal power harnessed from its ceaseless motion.

One develops an intuitive understanding of water's potential as an energy source, just as Norse speakers may have when viewing fjord bound waterfalls toppling to their depths. This rune, for many, serves as a tangible symbol of the immense, untapped energy latent within Laguz. Just as the waterfall transforms kinetic energy into electricity, this rune can represent the vast reservoirs of potential power residing within individuals and the world around them, untapped, waiting to be channeled.

Ingwaz: Growth And Potential

The name "Ing" is closely linked to the Norse god Freyr. In fact, one of his titles is "Yngvi-Freyr". The Ynglings, a legendary Swedish royal dynasty, claimed descent from Yngvi-Freyr, establishing a direct lineage between the god and earthly kingship. Ingwaz therefore is representative of the Norse deity linked to fertility, abundance, and the harvest, suggesting the concept of potential and growth. It symbolizes the seed that carries within it the blueprint for a new life. Just as a seed requires specific conditions to germinate and flourish, so too does human potential need nurturing and the right environment to manifest. This rune is a reminder that within each of us lies a spark of creativity and power waiting to be ignited.

It can signify the fertilization of an idea or project, or even where one is planting and spending most of their energy. It may herald a period of growth, both personal and professional. The visual representation of Ingwaz often takes the form of a diamond or a helix like esthetic. The diamond shape can be seen as a symbol of the potential contained within, while the helix represents the energy and drive needed to manifest and fertilize that potential.

Othala:Ancestors And Heritage

While "heritage" or "inherited estate or possessions " is the Proto-Germanic translation for Othala, oral traditions associate this rune with the ancestors.

Othala encapsulates a profound connection to one's roots, both in a physical and spiritual sense. It represents the land, the homestead, and all that is inherited. Symbolizing the physical and tangible assets passed down through generations, such as property and possessions, Othala also represents the unseen inherited traits of genetics. Special talents and abilities in addition to property and possessions are seen as valuable treasures from our familial bonds.

It is a reminder of the lineage from which we come and the collective experiences that have shaped our identity. It signifies not only the physical dwelling place but also the sense of belonging and security that comes with it. Othala encourages us to cultivate a strong foundation and create a nurturing environment for ourselves and our loved ones. It is a symbol of stability and continuity, reminding us of the importance of preserving our heritage for future generations. Inversely, we can also inherit negative traits and thought patterns from those in our lineage. For good or ill, Othala embodies the intangible inheritances: cultural traditions, family values, and ancestral wisdom.

From a spiritual perspective it is connected to the concept of ancestral spirits and the wisdom that can be gained from connecting with those who came before us. This rune invites us to delve into our family history, to learn from the successes and failures of our ancestors, and to draw inspiration from their lives. It can serve as a reminder of our inherent potential and the resources available to us. It encourages us to tap into our inner strength and utilize the gifts we have been given.

Dagaz: Dawn Of A New Day

Translated as "day," Dagaz embodies its spirit: the transition from darkness to light, from ignorance to enlightenment. Dagaz represents the dawning of a new era. It symbolizes the end of one cycle and the beginning of another, a period of profound change and growth. This rune is not merely about the physical dawn of a new day but also the spiritual awakening of consciousness. It signifies the moment when we shed the shadows of the past and embrace the potential of the future. This rune can herald new beginnings, breakthroughs, and the realization of one's full potential. The dawn of a new day implies that darkness is over. Nighttime has dissipated and less stressful, anxious times are ahead. With every passing hour new illumination grows leading us into a brighter future.

For many, Dagaz is associated with balance and harmony. The rune's symmetrical form suggests the importance of finding equilibrium between opposing forces. It is a reminder that light cannot exist without darkness, and that both are essential components of life's tapestry.

Just as your life is a tapestry woven from personal threads, so too is your relationship with the runes. As this bond strengthens, the runes will offer insights tailored to your soul's path in this world. Though rooted in tradition, their wisdom is a dynamic force, adaptable to your evolving experience. Your journey with the runes is a personal odyssey. As you deepen your connection to these archaic symbols, they will unveil their wisdom in a manner as singular and profound as your own life trajectory. While respecting their historical context, allow the runes to illuminate your unique perspective.

CHAPTER 7: CULTIVATING A RELATIONSHIP WITH THE ELDER FUTHARK RUNES

The Hávamál imparts a clear directive to comprehend the runes, yet the precise nature of this understanding remains elusive. The runes hold a profound allure for many. Beyond their historical significance, they offer a potential pathway to deeper self-understanding and connection with the natural world. Cultivating a personal relationship with these symbols requires a blend of reverence, study, and experiential learning.

Much of this learning is intuitive. This requires the learner to have a secure understanding of one's own intuition. The initial step towards establishing a connection with the Elder Futhark is a deep-seated respect for their history and cultural context. Familiarizing oneself with the history and culture they come from is not only necessary, but paramount to understanding their true essence. I cannot stress this enough.

We know that in addition to being a writing system, runes carried spiritual and magical significance. Understanding their role in Norse mythology and the lives of our ancestors can provide a rich foundation for personal interpretation. Become acquainted with Old Norse texts, literature and poetry as this is foundational in your understanding. It is essential to approach the runes with humility, recognizing that they are a tool for personal growth, not a magic wand.

Once a foundational understanding is established, the next step involves a thorough study of the runes themselves. As said in previous chapters, each rune possesses its own unique energy and meaning. There are countless books, articles, and online resources dedicated to rune interpretation. However, it is crucial to find resources that resonate with your personal beliefs and intuition. Some practitioners prefer a traditional, scholarly approach, while others lean towards a more modern, psychological interpretation. The key is to find a method that feels authentic and meaningful to you, while still keeping the explanations as unadulterated as possible.

Meditation and visualization can be powerful tools in developing a personal relationship with the runes. By focusing on a specific rune, you can explore its energy and symbolism on a deeper level. Imagine yourself as the essence of the rune, experiencing its shape, sound, and meaning. This practice can lead to profound insights and personal revelations expanding on traditional meanings. Journaling your experiences with each rune can also be beneficial. Writing down your thoughts and feelings can help to clarify your understanding and identify patterns in your relationship with the runes.

To truly embody the energy of the runes, it is indispensable to incorporate them into your daily life. In very plain speak, spend time with them. Carrying a rune stone, wearing rune jewelry, or creating rune-inspired art can help to maintain a conscious connection with these symbols. Some practitioners find it helpful to perform rune castings or divination for their own personal guidance and use, but it is important to remember that the runes are a tool for self-reflection, not necessarily prediction. The most valuable insights often come from exploring the nuances of the runes in relation to your own life experiences.

Nature is intimately connected to the runes. Spending time outdoors, observing the natural world, and connecting with the elements can deepen your understanding of the rune's energies. You will begin to see the runes in nature. Every rock, every tree will begin to present itself to you in this way. Many runes are associated with specific natural phenomena, such as animals, or celestial bodies. By immersing yourself in nature, you can gain a more profound appreciation for the rune's symbolism.

Building a relationship with the Elder Futhark runes is a journey, not a destination. It is a practice that requires a lifetime. It demands patience, dedication, and an open mind. There will be times of deep connection and understanding, as well as periods of confusion and doubt. Trust the process and allow the runes to reveal their wisdom in their own time. By approaching the runes with reverence, curiosity, and a willingness to learn, you can embark on a transformative path of heightened self-discovery and spiritual growth.

THE HAVAMAL
AS A GUIDE TO RUNE CONNECTION

Just as Óðin exhorts us to master the runes in the Hávamál stanza 144, let us use each line of his counsel as a roadmap to cultivating a profound connection and relationship with these primitive symbols. The following advice is my own interpretation of his admonitions in the Hávamál.

Do you know how to carve them?

Admonition: This refers to the physical act of creating runes. It suggests a deep connection with the material world and the tactile process of inscribing the characters.

Connection: To truly understand the runes, one must engage with them physically. Carving them can be a meditative practice, allowing for a personal connection with each rune. This involves spending time with them through a physical medium such as carving or writing.

Do you know how to read them?

Admonition: This implies understanding the meanings and interpretations associated with the runes. It involves the intellectual and intuitive aspects of rune work.

Connection: Reading the runes is about communication. It's about learning to listen to the wisdom they offer and developing an ability to interpret their messages as well as familiarizing oneself with their history.

Do you know how to blood them?

Admonition: This is a more esoteric practice, often involving the application of blood to the runes to activate their power. It signifies a deep personal commitment and connection.

Connection: Blooding the runes can be seen as a sacred act, symbolizing a profound bond and sacrifice. It's a way to infuse the runes with personal energy and intention. Many folk practices, including Scandinavian magical traditions, view saliva and spit as effective as blood.

Do you know how to test them?

Admonition: This suggests the need to experiment with the runes to understand their workings. It involves observation, trial, and error.

Connection: Testing the runes is a learning process. It's about gaining practical experience and building trust in their guidance. This again involves a time commitment of working with the runes in your everyday life.

Do you know how to invoke them?

Admonition: This refers to the ability to call upon the power of the runes for specific purposes. It involves ritual and focus.

Connection: Invoking the runes is about establishing a working relationship. It's about learning to harness their energy for desired outcomes. In this way, viewing the runes as spiritual energies or guides is helpful and produces a deeper meaning.

Do you know how to blót?

Admonition: Blót is a Norse sacrificial ritual. Here, it likely refers to offerings made to the runes as a form of worship or gratitude.

Connection: Blót is a way to honor the runes and show respect for their power. It's about giving back and nurturing the relationship. Offerings are an integral way to perform blót. One a spiritual perspective takes place then blót is the next logical development in the relationship.

Do you know how to cast them?

Admonition: This admonition is often interpreted as casting out or sending forth the runes to be used magically, spiritually, or for healing purposes. However, I believe it could also refer to the art of casting runes with the intention of divination. The later would involve asking questions and interpreting the resulting spread.

Connection: Casting the runes is a form of communication and consultation. It's about seeking guidance and learning to trust the insights offered. It's the investigation of counsel given from the runes. We will explore this in the next chapter.

Do you know how to sacrifice them?

Admonition: A source of debate among scholars and practitioners of Norse traditions, it's important to approach this line with respect and caution. This is the most challenging line to interpret without further context. It likely refers to a deep, sacrificial aspect of rune work, perhaps symbolizing letting go or transformation.

Connection: Understanding this line requires careful consideration and might involve exploring personal symbolism and deep shadow work. This interpretation suggests a symbolic sacrifice. It might refer to relinquishing attachments or preconceived notions to gain deeper insights, suggesting a profound dedication to the runes, perhaps involving a significant personal sacrifice or commitment to the path of rune work.

The Hávamál outlines a comprehensive path to developing a deep and meaningful relationship with the runes. It suggests a journey of physical engagement, intellectual understanding, spiritual connection, and practical application.

Remember, the most authentic connection to the runes comes from within. Authenticity is the foundation for any healthy relationship. While external resources can provide valuable guidance, the true meaning of the runes is ultimately revealed through your own experiences and interpretations. Trust your intuition, and allow the runes to become a source of inspiration and empowerment in your life.

CHAPTER EIGHT: RUNE CASTING

"To divination and casting of lots, they [the Germanic tribes] pay attention beyond any other people. Their method of casting lots is a simple one: they cut a branch from a fruit-bearing tree and divide it into small pieces which they mark with certain distinctive signs and scatter at random onto a white cloth. Then, the priest of the community if the lots are consulted publicly, or the father of the family if it is done privately, after invoking the gods and with eyes raised to heaven, picks up three pieces, one at a time, and interprets them according to the signs previously marked upon them."
-Tacitus, in Chapter X of his Germania (circa 98 AD)

Similar to Tacitus's writing above, Rimbert writes about a divination practice among Danish peoples observed by Anskar, the Frankish bishop and missionary in the Vita Ansgarii (869-876 AD.)

The story unfolds as Anskar and Rimbert were traveling through Sweden, spreading the Christian faith. One day, they encountered a Swedish man who was seeking guidance from a diviner. This practice, common among the Norse people, involved consulting with individuals believed to have supernatural powers to predict the future or gain insights into hidden knowledge. The man, troubled that he may have offended a god, consulted the soothsayer, who casted lots to identify the aggrieved deity. The men believed that casting lots could determine which deity, whether Christian or Norse, had issue with the man and what to do about it. Rimbert describes the scene: "A man, skilled in the arts of divination, was standing before the people, casting lots. He held in his hand a vessel filled with small, round stones. He would shake the vessel and then draw out a stone. The outcome of the divination depended on which stone was chosen."

While the above surviving historical records provide insufficient evidence to definitively state that runes were the specific symbols employed in their lot-casting practices, it is evident from contemporary accounts that divination was a central purpose of the lots cast by Germanic peoples. These observations, made by outsiders to Northern European cultures, underscore the significance of these practices in their societies and belief systems.

This chapter delves into the art of rune casting, as potentially observed in Scandinavian and Germanic cultures. It will provide a comprehensive guide to the process, the intricate relationships between the runes, and the nuanced interpretation of readings. While the practice of rune casting has ancient roots in oral traditions, it's important to acknowledge that our contemporary understanding and methods have evolved significantly. This presentation aims to foster a deeper appreciation for the Elder Futhark and its practical application in modern life. It also seeks to illuminate the ancestral belief in the power of divination to connect with the divine, nature, and one's own destiny.

The interpretation of runes is complex and often relies on the rune master's knowledge, intuition, and the context of the questions asked. While employing the unique symbols of a runic alphabet, practitioners seek insights into the complexities of life, exploring both the present moment and potential future paths. This form of divination typically involves casting or tossing runes—often small stones or wood pieces inscribed with the runic characters—in various methods. Some practitioners prefer to throw the runes onto a flat surface, interpreting their scattered positions as a cosmic map. Others opt for a more deliberate approach, drawing runes from a pouch. Regardless of the method, the arrangement of the runes is believed to offer a symbolic meaning, revealing hidden patterns and potentialities. It's essential to dispel the misconception of rune casting as mere fortune-telling. While it can provide glimpses into future possibilities, its primary function is to offer guidance and understanding.

By illuminating the underlying forces at play, runes empower individuals to make informed decisions and navigate life's challenges with greater clarity and purpose. Rune casting serves as a powerful tool for introspection and problem-solving, tapping into the subconscious mind to illuminate potential outcomes. By focusing on a particular challenge or decision, individuals can harness the wisdom of the runes to gain clarity and perspective.

Old Norse people relied on omens, messages from the gods revealed through nature, to predict the future. These practices are detailed in the sagas. They believed that the flight of birds, the gallop of horses, or even extraordinary celestial events like solar eclipses held divine significance. While distancing ourselves from the false claims and narratives of the last century, it is still plausible to assume that runes, also seen as connected to the natural world and expressions of natural phenomena, were also likely employed in divination.

Modern rune casting often blends historical knowledge with personal intuition. While not strictly adhering to the enigmatic ancient methods, these contemporary practices can offer insights into the potential divinatory uses of runes in the past.

Rune casting is an art, a multifaceted practice, with diverse techniques ranging from directional alignments to the symbolic significance and diversity of casting cloths. While historical references to these methods are scant, beyond a fleeting mention of a "white piece of cloth," the absence of a standardized approach underscores the rich tapestry of individual and cultural interpretations. In light of this, I will endeavor to share the methods I have been privileged to learn and subsequently impart to my students.

Step One: Consecrate hands and runes tools

Selecting the tools

The creation of your rune set is a deeply personal journey. Trust your intuition to guide you in this process. Many practitioners believe that crafting one's own rune set fosters a uniquely intimate connection with the symbols. This idea is rooted in the belief that a profound bond develops as you shape and form each individual piece.

While there's flexibility in the materials you choose, opting for natural elements is often preferred. These materials are believed to retain a resonance with the Earth's natural energy. By carving or shaping runes from these elements, practitioners suggest that you're tapping into this inherent spiritual vitality, infusing your runes with a potent and authentic energy.

Wood is a classic choice for rune crafting due to its malleability and ease of carving. Its connection to the natural world evokes imagery of the Norns, ancient Norse fate-weavers, who are often depicted carving the wood roots at the base of the World Tree, Yggdrasil.

Stone, shells, and bone are other popular mediums, each offering unique qualities. Many runecrafters, myself included, enjoy the process of collecting special pieces over time, allowing a deeper connection to form between the material and the intended rune. This thoughtful approach infuses the runes with personal significance.

While crafting your own rune set is often encouraged for fostering a deep personal connection, it's essential to dispel the notion that purchased sets cannot offer the same depth of interaction. Many beautifully crafted rune sets are available from skilled artisans, imbued with care and reverence for the ancient symbols. I personally own a set created by a renowned West Coast artist, and I've found its energy to be profound and impactful in my readings with clients.

For those unable to craft their own set, runes made from quartz or resin can be equally potent tools. The true value of a rune set doesn't lie solely in its origin but in the relationship you build with it. As we'll explore in the section on consecration, the energy you invest in your runes is paramount to their effectiveness.

CONSECRATION

Consecration, the act of making something sacred or holy, was a fundamental ritual in many ancient cultures. This process is particularly important for tools, especially those used in spiritual or ceremonial practices. These tools, whether simple or complex, are and were believed to serve as intermediaries between the human and divine realms.

The primary reason for consecrating tools is to imbue them with divine or spiritual energy. This power is believed to enhance the tool's efficacy and purpose. Consecration, also a purification ritual, removes any negative or mundane energies from the tool. This ensures that it is a pure vessel for sacred work, forging a connection between the tool, its user, and the divine. This bond is essential for effective spiritual practices. When cleansing a tool with water, fire, or smoke, some cultures use herbs or salt for purification. I recommend using tjärved (tar wood) or juniper bundles as sustainable alternatives to popular cleansing tools like palo santo and white sage. Due to concerns about overharvesting, many indigenous communities have raised awareness about the unsustainable practices surrounding these plants and trees. Employing tools native to a specific tradition, whenever possible, helps connect us to the ancestral roots of that practice.

Tjärved is a type of smoke wand used in Nordic folk magic. Often referred to as "poor people's candles," tjärved is made from pine branches that have died and developed a high resin content. This natural resin makes them burn slowly and produce a fragrant smoke. Juniper is an evergreen coniferous plant that thrives in colder climates. It can be easily gathered and bound into a smoke cleansing bundle.

The application of sacred oils or other substances is also believed to impart specific properties to our tools. Oils, often infused with herbs or charged with specific intentions, act as a conduit for spiritual energy. As the oil is applied, practitioners may visualize the desired outcome or recite prayers, incantations, or invocations to call upon divine or spiritual forces to bless the objects.

It is important to note that the hands are indispensable instruments in any practitioner's arsenal, particularly for divination. Before engaging in healing or rune work, I take a moment to purify and consecrate my hands by washing and anointing them as they serve as conduits for my subconscious and soul energy. Sometimes sacred tools are dedicated to a specific deity or purpose. In some traditions, tools might be buried or hidden for a period of time, symbolizing rebirth or transformation. I recommend burying store bought rune sets in the Earth for a designated time before the consecration process. I believe this ritual clears energetic blockages and allows the Earth's positive healing energy to be absorbed by the runes. While this effect is purely subjective, I've found it to be beneficial in my practice.

Understanding the significance of consecration gives us insight into the reverence and care with which instruments should be treated and help us to approach them with a deeper sense of purpose and respect.

STEP TWO: CREATE THE SACRED SPACE

Once cleansing and consecration are complete, it's beneficial to cleanse the casting area as well. While not always feasible, this additional purification can be helpful. Regardless of location, transforming your surroundings, whether large or small, into a consecrated area invites spiritual energies to converge. This dedicated space should be a welcoming sanctuary that resonates with your personal power. By creating such an environment, you establish a focused and potent arena for your casting.

There are a variety of opinions on the ideal casting surface. Cloths may have bindrunes or Old Norse imagery on them while some practitioners may prefer to only cast directly on the ground. Tacitus noted Germanic tribes casted on white cloth when divining, a practice upheld in my trolldom tradition. Personally, I often use light or white rabbit fur for this purpose though I have used other fabric and textiles as well with just as much success.

There's a compelling parallel between the high seat in seiðr and the runic casting cloth in divination. Both signify the creation of a sacred space inviting the otherworldly. A "setting apart" transforms the ordinary into the extraordinary, giving the space a marked distinction, or boundary. This connection threads together another concept in Old Norse speaker's minds: hospitality. Similar to how Old Norse culture exalted hospitality, their divinatory practices also emphasized a welcoming approach. The concept of inviting spirits into one's space was integral to their rituals.

Step Three: Ask, Connect

A practice passed down through my familial lineage, and one I've yet to encounter elsewhere, involves offering a supplication or prayer prior to casting. With the ritual space prepared, I internally connect with my ancestors, landvættir (land spirits), and the energy of the runes. Calling forth the ancestors is most important. Often, they can bring messages and information from other realms which is extremely helpful. They also add an element of protection during the reading.

I recommend humbly asking ancestors that you have built a connection with to be present. I then vocalize a clear request for guidance in interpreting the forthcoming rune cast. This action serves multiple purposes: it aligns my subconscious with the intent, informs the involved spirits and energies, and engages the client's attention, focusing their mind on the reading. Ultimately belief in one's own abilities and ancestral guidance is all that is required here.

Step Four: Cast Interpretations And Alignments

Given the diversity of rune casting methods, I'll share my personal approach. I love to cast from a snapping turtle shell. Turtles have a particular connection to me, though turtles in general are not native to Scandinavia and haven't been so for approximately 5,000 years. Many practitioners prefer to use leather pouches. Assuming the container has undergone the aforementioned consecration, I, with great intention, lightly toss the runes from the shell onto my white fur casting cloth. I then begin to remove the runes that are not speaking or sharing during that cast. This is evidenced by those runes that are turned upside-down. I remove them, placing them back in the turtle shell and set it aside.

I typically begin my reading by focusing on the runes at the center of the casting cloth or fur. This central cluster often encapsulates the core of the issues at hand, while peripheral runes provide additional context or explanatory details, radiating out away from the center.

Although I generally don't assign directional significance to my casting plane, some practitioners correlate the four cardinal directions with the cloth's orientation. This practice is also reflected in Scandinavian folk practice traditions, where specific attributes, spirits, and elements are associated with each direction.

As runes will naturally cluster when cast, I interpret these groupings as sentences. To decipher these, a deep understanding of each rune's literal and symbolic meaning is crucial. Comprehensive knowledge of the rune's whole spectrum, favorable and inversely unfavorable characteristics, as anything could possibly come into play depending on where each rune is grouped.

One must mentally construct words, phrases, and sentence structures while simultaneously listening for insights from external forces, reading the cast as a paragraph.

Unlike most rune readers, I do not rely on upright or inverted positions for interpretation. While others often draw or cast three runes, as described by Tacitus in The Germania, my approach is different. I have developed this method independently, solely under my father's guidance. This alludes to the diversity of this rich tradition. Scandinavians in particular were very isolated geographically and developed individual ways to connect to their folk practices. From teacher to student, esoteric traditions were pollinated and bore fruit with each subsequent generation.

Once, having a sense of what spirits are showing me, I will address each topic with the inquisitor. Often, people are surprised by the information they receive. What they initially sought is overshadowed by the knowledge and guidance they truly needed to hear. Spiritual and emotional knots are untangled and Inner turmoil is resolved.

Other points to note are runes that land in peculiar positions during the cast. Runes that are off the mat may imply a future event taking place. Those that fly across a table or land far out of the realm of the expected casting are of particular importance and should be acknowledged as such during the reading. One can surmise a conclusion by sensing the energy given from that particular rune and its denotation.

With practice, these techniques will become instinctive, guided by the insights gained through experience.

You will begin to see the subtleties of how each rune is affected and interacts with one another developing your own intuitive interpretations. Casting is an ocular divinatory method whose main impetus is to give guidance and counsel. Ultimately, the application of this knowledge rests in the hands of its recipients.

STEP FIVE: SHOW RESPECT

Upon completing the reading, the runes should be returned to their storage place with reverence. I typically keep mine within their protective turtle shell, accompanied by a black kyanite crystal. Renowned for its energy-cleansing properties, the kyanite helps to maintain the purity of the runes between readings. This practice ensures that the runes remain energetically clear and ready for their next use. Again this too is a subjective element that I have added. You may develop your own personal method of clearing your tools.

Now that the casting is concluded, it is essential to express gratitude and reverence for the runes themselves and the spiritual entities that have participated. Often, I feel compelled to offer a token of appreciation to those spirits who have been particularly helpful or insightful during the casting. Just as in any meaningful relationship, a reciprocal exchange of energy and respect is vital to maintaining a harmonious connection with the spiritual realm.

Gratitude and proper care are fundamental to a meaningful and effective rune practice. By honoring the spirits involved, cleansing and creating a sacred space for the runes, one cultivates a deep connection to the ancient wisdom they hold.

CHAPTER 9: GOING BEYOND
RUNES AS PORTALS AND CONDUITS

Runes As Portals

While some believe runes mirror the cosmic axis mundi—the symbolic pillar connecting heaven, earth, and the underworld— this view is not universally accepted and to many is considered a product of contemporary thought.

One could argue though that the concept of runes as portals to accessing guidance is actually rooted in their linguistic and mythological context. The significance of language to societies built on oral transmission is immeasurable.

Old Norse, a direct descendant of Proto-Germanic, the language in which runes were primarily used, is rich in poetic and metaphorical expressions. Words themselves were perceived as possessing intrinsic power, capable of shaping reality.

Poetry was paramount in Old Norse society, serving as the cornerstone of their oral tradition. Skalds, the masters of this art, wielded immense power and prestige, often employed by kings and law makers. Through their verses, they preserved genealogies, history, and myths, shaping the cultural identity of the people.

Runes, as the fundamental building blocks of language, were naturally endowed with similar potency. Furthermore, the act of writing itself was considered a sacred process. Runes were formidable forces that could influence events and individuals. The creation of a runic inscription was akin to casting a spell, with the runes acting as intermediaries between the human world and the divine or spiritual realms.

The Cosmic Axis Mundi Is a fundamental cosmological concept in many mythologies often symbolized by a world tree, a mountain, or a pillar.

In Norse mythology, the world tree, Yggdrasil, is depicted as connecting the nine realms. It is conceivable that runes, as linguistic constructs, could be seen as microcosmic representations of this cosmic axis, offering pathways to traverse the different planes of existence. I personally believe runes were used for divination, predicting possible outcomes of future events or understanding the present situation. This practice implies an ability to access information from different planes of existence, much like the cosmic axis provides a conduit between worlds.

Imperatively, each rune has a specific sound value and often an esoteric association. This duality reflects the idea that the physical world (sound) is connected to a spiritual or metaphysical world (association). It could suggest a bridge between the material and the divine.

In some interpretations, the creation of the world is linked to the creation of language and writing. The runes, as the building blocks of language, could then be seen as participating in the cosmic order and creation.

Lastly, Runes were often used in personal rituals or meditations. By working with runes, individuals could embark on a journey of self-discovery, transformation, and journeying, mirroring the individual's path through the different planes of existence. By viewing runes through this lens, they become potent tools for understanding the universe and one's place within it. Runes offer a framework for exploring the relationship between the human experience and the cosmic order, suggesting that language itself is a sacred and powerful force.

Runes As Conduits

The idea of runes as conduits for ancestral knowledge is deeply intertwined with the Norse concept of fate (Wyrd). Wyrd was believed to be an immutable force that determined the course of events, shaped by the actions of both gods and humans. Runes, as carriers of information and meaning, were seen as repositories of collective memory.

The Norse concept of the Web of Wyrd is a powerful metaphor for understanding fate and destiny in their mythology. It depicts life as an intricate tapestry woven by the Norns, three powerful goddesses associated with destiny, fate and the ancestors. Let's review our previous observation of the Norns. Urðr: The past, representing the wellspring of fate, Verdandi: The present, shaping the current moment and Skuld: The future, determining what will or what ought to be.

These goddesses reside at the base of the World Tree, where they continuously weave the threads of fate, influencing the lives of gods and mortals alike. The Web of Wyrd symbolizes the interconnectedness of all things. Every action, every decision, and every event is a thread woven into the grand tapestry of existence. The past, present, and future are not linear but intertwined, creating a complex pattern of cause and effect. This is a profound worldview, emphasizing the acceptance of fate, yet the possibility to change it. The Web of Wyrd continues to resonate with modern audiences as a symbol of the complexity of life, the interplay between choice and destiny, and the importance of living in harmony with the natural world. While the Norns determine the overall pattern of life, individuals still possess agency. The Norse believed in the importance of personal accountability, choices, and actions which could influence the specific path taken within the broader framework of fate, even affecting one's future generations and offspring.

Representing the delicate balance of the universe, disrupting the balance of the Web of Wyrd could have far-reaching consequences.

The potential role of runes as portals and conduits is further illuminated when considered within a shamanic framework. I use the word "shamanism" here as a descriptive word characteristic of a widespread belief system characterized by trance states and spirit journeying. This practice was likely prevalent among the Norse people. The use of rhythmic patterns and sounds in shamanic practices is reminiscent of the poetic and alliterative structure of old Norse language. Runes, with their inherent sonic qualities, could perhaps have been employed to induce trance states and to establish a connection with the spirit world. It is possible they may have been used as tools to facilitate these altered states of consciousness, enabling shamans to access otherworldly realms and communicate with spirits. As we have no evidence of shamanic practices apart from seiðr in texts and grave burials, the concept of runes as a reflection of the cosmic axis mundi through a shamanic lens is still only conjecture.

While the idea that Norse runes functioned as portals and conduits for ancestral knowledge is speculative, it is a compelling hypothesis. By exploring the intersection of language, mythology, and shamanism, we gain a deeper appreciation for the multifaceted nature of these ancient symbols.

The runes, as both linguistic and spiritual tools, offer a window into the worldview of the Norse people. They represent a bridge between the material and spiritual realms, inviting us to contemplate the possibility of hidden dimensions and the enduring wisdom of our ancestors.

CONCLUSION

I hope your journey through the Elder Futhark and the principles of rune casting have been a catalyst to rediscover your innate connection to the natural world. While our bonds have been gradually eroded by the relentless march of consumerism, by delving into the heart of rune lore, I hope you have unearthed a profound understanding of the interconnectedness of all beings. This worldview reveres the Earth as a living entity and recognizes our role as its stewards.

The runes, the language of the cosmos, help us communicate with the natural world, listen to its wisdom, and to align our lives with its rhythms. By embracing an animistic perspective, we can cultivate a deeper sense of purpose and belonging, and begin to dismantle the materialistic systems that have alienated us from ourselves, the planet, and one another.

This book is not a definitive guide but a starting point. The runes are a tool for personal exploration and growth. It's my desire that by sharing these insights, they inspire readers to embark on their own journeys of rediscovery. Let's reclaim our ancestral wisdom, nurture harmonious relationships with the Earth, eachother, and build a future where human flourishing and ecological well-being are inseparable. The time for change is now. The runes await.

Karin Dahlström (Rune Guidance Of The Norse) is runic practitioner who teaches an animistic worldview from a Norse perspective. Having a professional past in art & design, she is now a mentor & speaker on old Norse spirituality and its benefits and place in our world today. With a focus on spiritual counseling & divination, Karin is a teacher and mentor in old Scandinavian folk practices. As an educator of the art of rune casting, much of the information in this book she learned during her many visits to Sweden visiting family & friends. Karin also has spiritual counseling and healing practice located in her metaphysical shop, Alchemy Rumes located on the Caloosahatchee river in SW Florida where she resides with her family & two cats.

The Three Little Sisters

The Three Little Sisters is an indie publisher that puts authors first. We specialize in the strange and unusual. From titles about pagan and heathen spirituality to traditional fiction we bring books to life.

https://shop.the3littlesisters.com

www.ingramcontent.com/pod-product-compliance
Lightning Source LLC
Chambersburg PA
CBHW060954120626
46557CB00003B/1162